T0193364

In *Lifting the Veil,* one cries, laughs, and smiles as the chapters unfold because one can identify with all of the emotions. At the end, love and faith prevail.

- Eva Alejandro, college educator, business owner

LIFTING THE
VEIL

A MEMOIR

S.S. SIMPSON

authorHOUSE®

AuthorHouse™
1663 Liberty Drive
Bloomington, IN 47403
www.authorhouse.com
Phone: 1 (800) 839-8640

© *2020 S.S. Simpson. All rights reserved.*

No part of this book may be reproduced, stored in a retrieval system, or transmitted by any means without the written permission of the author.

Published by AuthorHouse 12/17/2019

ISBN: 978-1-7283-4004-3 (sc)
ISBN: 978-1-7283-4014-2 (e)

Print information available on the last page.

Any people depicted in stock imagery provided by Getty Images are models, and such images are being used for illustrative purposes only. Certain stock imagery © Getty Images.

This book is printed on acid-free paper.

Because of the dynamic nature of the Internet, any web addresses or links contained in this book may have changed since publication and may no longer be valid. The views expressed in this work are solely those of the author and do not necessarily reflect the views of the publisher, and the publisher hereby disclaims any responsibility for them.

DEDICATION

I dedicate *Lifting the Veil* to my loving mother and co-editor, who has always believed in me. I am grateful for your support, encouragement, and the countless hours you spent helping me polish my book.

IN AN INSTANT

Drenched, I had just finished directing traffic, most of which came from the football game that had just let out moments before. An hour earlier the unsteadiness in Papa's voice unnerved me. It was a very brief phone call requesting help from Samuel and me. But Papa never needed help, so Samuel and I left immediately, scurrying out of the house, forgetting to kiss Mama goodbye. Part of me wished that I were still home, enjoying Mama's pampering and finishing up last-minute packing––stuffing needed school items into two unwilling backseats of my inherited fifty Ford. Two short days from now, I would be headed back to the university for my last year of pharmacy classes. But tonight Papa had assigned me traffic control, and now I needed to concentrate on what lay directly thirty feet ahead of me. An unfortunate truck had been swallowed by a water-logged ditch and couldn't be budged. Samuel and Papa were frantically trying to fasten a towing harness under the belly of the submerged pick-up truck as young Tito, who was Papa's co-pilot on service calls, peered cautiously from a distance. Usually Papa performed this task flawlessly because he had twenty years of experience working as a night wrecker service operator for Best Motors. But tonight, tonight was different. He was physically struggling with the overturned vehicle that was anchored in the mud like a cemented flagpole. Thinking aloud, I wondered why he answered the motorist's call, tonight of all nights. Yet I

1

knew why. Papa was needed and responded. As cars crept closer and closer to me, I wished he didn't always have to be so responsible. But being Papa's son, I was right beside him, making the best of an unnerving situation. It had to be genetic, I decided, watching a car whirl by, which emptied a submerged pothole and showered me with its contents. Then I heard it.

"Look out, it's coming right at you, jump!" the screaming voice called out. Out of the corner of my eye, I suddenly saw it and, jumping with every ounce of energy that I had, lifted up both of my legs, although it wasn't fast enough or high enough. Feeling cold wet metal slice into my right leg, I watched my body being hurtled through the air as if viewing the latest take of an experienced stuntman, but then I heard the loud thundering thud as I hit the solid ground on the opposite side of the road. Landing in wet muddy gravel, I then knew that it was my own leg. Feeling intense saturating pain, I reached down to where it was throbbing uncontrollably, trying to stop the bleeding, but much to my horror it wasn't there. Feeling sure I was mistaken, I groped again but only grabbed a handful of bloody gravel, which bit defiantly into my right hand. Sensing things were much more critical than I had possibly thought, I knew that if I didn't stop the bleeding, it would stop me. With that dreadful thought taunting me, I somehow managed to rip off the tattered right sleeve of my shirt, turning it into a makeshift tourniquet while wrapping it around what was now left of my right leg. When I yelled as loudly as I could, the silence of my own voice terrified me, hearing only gasps of air. As I pressed down on clumps of soft mangled tissue held together with clumps of bloody flesh, I felt my flesh slip between my fingers like pieces of raw meat. Blood surrounded me, squirting into the air like a macabre water fountain, but suddenly all I could feel was Papa's warm trembling hand on my drenched forehead while he softly agonized, convincing himself that this was all his fault.

Feeling his wet tears on my cheeks as he cradled me in his arms, my inner spirit moaned. I then decided that I wasn't going to die. If for no other reason, I wasn't going to leave him, and I wanted only to stop his sobbing.

In the tangled background, I heard Samuel's shouting, "Is he dead? He's dead."

Poor Samuel, always imagining the worst. Trying to halt his fear by answering him, I opened my mouth but only gasped as empty sounds rushed out. Shock was beginning to win, overtaking me, but I fought to stay awake, knowing that if I didn't, I would bleed to death. Slowly Papa's reassuring grip grappled with the tourniquet, so I let myself go bit by bit, hoping that he would know what to do. Floating in and out of consciousness, I could hear Papa instructing a terrified, wide-eyed Tito to go and get some help wherever he could find it. Trembling with an unaccustomed fear at seeing me helpless, Tito quickly leaned over, touched my cold cheek, assured me he would be back with help, and departed without glancing back.

"Son, everything will be all right, just know that," I heard Papa softly murmur, praying to his powerful God to allow me to live, offering his own life in exchange for mine. While Papa prayed I felt a strange calmness overtake me as though the good Lord might intervene, allowing me to live despite the overwhelming odds. As Papa held me, I realized how much I meant to him, although he never felt comfortable telling me until then.

"Polo, I love you very much, although rarely do I ever tell you," Papa said softly. "You have made me so very proud, being the first in our family to go to college and make something of yourself." Choking on his words, he paused, knowing that he only had a few moments to tell me what he had been feeling for too many years. "You have a gift, the gift to learn and the drive to achieve, which is something that I never had. You have my stubbornness but Mama's inner will to fight, so I want you to use it now because this is your most important fight."

Stroking my hair, Papa heavily heaved and softly said, "Son, I will never leave you; so please don't leave me. When Papa finished he knew that if there were any chance at all, help needed to come quickly. Just as his hope had faded away, a siren split the night air, filling it with anxious alarm; then I allowed myself to let go completely. Two young, experienced paramedics donned in impeccable, white uniforms pounced out of nowhere, startling Papa like a frightened rabbit. Taking command of the situation, one of them carefully wrapped what was left of my leg with a mound of sterile dressing, covering it with constricting tape. The other one artfully flicked a needle into my arm, confidently secured me on a gurney, and slipped me into the ambulance, along with Samuel, who had also been hit by the same unwieldy car. By the sound of Samuel's bellowing, you would think that he was the unlucky legless victim. Even as a young boy, he couldn't handle any pain, and tonight was no exception with his two broken ribs, a broken shoulder, and a bruised pelvis. He at least could be put back together again. With its valuable cargo, the siren once again shrieked into the darkness, knowing full well that nothing could get in its way since every minute counted.

Meanwhile, as Papa's fear slowly turned to anger, he saw the beat-up car that had violated both of his innocent sons. Getting stuck in the gooey mud, the car halted abruptly and out came a young, sputtering drunken man, cursing as he passed out, sprawling on the wet, unforgiving ground. Papa watched his fists rise slowly into the air ready to pound when a voice behind him said, "Sir, move away and let me take care of this."

Certain that he was hearing things, Papa turned around and gazed into a pair of enforcing eyes. It was a uniform-clad sheriff staring him down, having arrived only a few moments earlier.

"This man has taken everything away from me, crippling my son, probably killing him; he has to pay. Let me finish this the only fair way," burst Papa, crying out indignantly as the sheriff slowly put his arm around him, consoling him as though he were his own father.

"Sir, let me do what I need to do," the commanding voice answered while he quickly snapped a pair of flashy, metal handcuffs onto the unsteady hands of the staggering drunk.

"What, what are you doing to me?" the slobbering, disheveled kid shouted as his intoxicated voice poisoned the night air. The sheriff shoved him into the backseat of his waiting vehicle, slammed the door, and quickly disappeared into the blackness of the night. Broken, Papa tried to make himself move, but he couldn't think; none of it made any sense. Was his son truly legless, lying helpless on a hospital gurney, wondering whether he would face death alone or with anyone who cared? The thought snapped him out of his numbness, and then he heard Tito cry out.

"Papa, the men with the white uniforms took..." But before he could finish, Papa was ready to fight his fight, needing to get to the hospital in time. With adrenalin raging through every pore in his body, he grabbed Tito and prayed speed would intervene. It did. Suddenly there he was beside me, shaking uncontrollably, clutching my fingers in his, not wanting to let go yet knowing that he had to. Dreading the call, he dialed, waited, and heard the quiet stillness of his wife's voice as he said, "It's both boys, but Polo ... something has happened; you need to come to the hospital as quickly as possible." He heard only stunned silence.

Sensing a weight that shifted from his shoulders, Papa then just waited, but not for very long. After what seemed only minutes, Papa heard a quivering voice from behind him tenderly whispering, "Polo, I'm here."

It was Mama. She gushed as she knelt by me, nearly collapsing, knowing that I was the only person in the world whom she couldn't and wouldn't live without. From deep within my soul, I heard these loving murmurings of sweetness and longing. Sensing that it was Mama, it somehow gave me the courage to face what lay before me. Death. But I had no regrets, because now I was not alone. She was here. But that courage was yanked from me when one of the emergency room doctors said, "Your boy is in good hands. You need to leave the rest up to us."

Papa tried to undo Mama's locked fingers from the chilly steel side rail of my stretcher. While Papa softly held her, she heaved with grief as everything that meant anything was being taken from her. Then all I felt were jabs as tubes were jammed simultaneously in every opening of my weary body. Bright lights and hurried voices surrounded me, and I waited for God to intervene, knowing I couldn't endure the pounding pain any longer where my right leg once was.

"Is he under?" an anxious voice called out. Straining, I opened my eyes one last time to protest then heard a very calm voice say, "I want you to count to ten," so I started counting and got as far as five, and then there was nothing but blank blackness. Listening for God's voice, I knew there was a fairly good chance that I had pleased him with my brief life, although there was that time ... But before I could come to any sound answer, I heard Mama's voice again, telling me to open my eyes. I decided I must be in heaven because Mama was too good to be anywhere else, and somehow she had managed to get a visitor's pass to help me get settled. When I opened my eyes, I was amazed; there were no heavenly angels but earthly ones, Mama and Papa. Slowly coming to, I instinctively reached down under the covers to see if my manhood had been spared. It had, even though there was nothing much to the right of it except bandages.

Again I heard that calm voice enter the room and watched the face that it belonged to.

"Son, you have lost your right leg, and we were not able to reattach it, but you still have a part of your upper leg, and with ..."

I didn't want to hear any more, deciding instead to drift back into my silent, blank blackness. Eventually faint whisperings awoke me, those voices I recognized and loved, forcing me out of my darkness.

"Enrique, how could this happen? It was terrible enough for Samuel to break his ribs, but they will mend. But Polo, he can't mend; there is nothing to mend. His determination, his promise that was his way out. What now, what now, now what will become of him? How can he survive? What have you done to my beloved Polo? Why did you have to insist that the boys help you? Why, why, why?" And with that final why, Mama's voice trailed off, utterly defeated.

"Marceline, I was wrong; it was wrong, but I didn't know; how could I have known?" Papa pleaded. "I would change places with him in an instant if I could. I know how much you love Polo, but I love him just as much and also had dreams for him. But now they have been snuffed out like the final rays of a brilliant autumn sunset on a brisk October's eve. Oh, my dear Marceline ... Who will want him now, being only half a man?" Papa wept as they embraced each other in lifeless arms. Screaming, I cried out, because now it didn't matter; nothing did; my angels had given up on me.

"No, no, Mama, Papa, I am still a man. No, no, I ..." My voice cut through the darkness like the cold metal that had severed my leg, leaving behind a lifeless stump that clung to me with uncertainty.

Yet suddenly a frantic voice filled my ears, drowning out my cries.

"Polo, Polo, wake up, I'm here." This figure was cradling me in her soft arms as I twisted in agony, unable to release my anguish, stubbornly refusing to give in to it.

"I am a man, I am a man, my leg, my leg," I sobbed, slowly waking up, gazing into a pair of tear-filled, questioning eyes, but the eyes had changed; the eyes belonged to someone who did want me. Papa was wrong; she was here with me now; and the eyes cared deeply, locking onto mine, pulling me out of that hospital room.

As Sara gently rocked me, it all started to make more sense. My worst nightmare had really happened, only thirty-five years ago to the day. Everything had changed in an unimaginable instant: the family's first college-graduate-to-be was transformed into a legless invalid whom everyone pitied. The accident's vice-like grip had squeezed almost every bit of life out of me thirty-five years ago, but now it seemed to want all of me.

Grabbing my throbbing stump, I suddenly felt pain, agonizing pain that saturated every nerve ending along its way, starting with my missing right toe on my missing right foot, inching upwards on my missing right leg, and ending in my shredded right stump, which was the only thing that was actually there. With each passing year, the pain seemed to be more unbearable, and tonight was no different. It was as though the pain grabbed all control, knew it, and wanted me, all of me, to suffer. To make matters worse, nobody really understood my pain since it rushed through a leg that wasn't even there. It was considered a mere case of mental gymnastics. Usually the advice given was just try not to think about it, which only infuriated me all the more. How could anyone possibly ignore knife-like shooting pain even though it wasn't supposed to be there? But I felt it all, every bit of it, and I couldn't stand it. Right now I just needed for Sara to know, to understand, why I was so broken and couldn't be fixed.

"It's the pain in my stump," I said softly. "I can't fight it. I just can't do it anymore; I am tired. It has taken everything from me, my life, my feelings, my dreams, and my ability to love." I wondered if there were any way Sara could make a connection with these unfamiliar words. Tragedy was absolutely foreign to her. She was a free spirit steered by a joyful soul.

"When it happened, everyone thought my life was over, including me." I paused, pouring out the gruesome details of that fateful night. Once admitted to the hospital, my horror just seemed to continue as countless unneeded operations were performed on me because the doctors were bound and determined to desensitize the nerve centers in my stump. They couldn't and finally stopped, leaving only five inches of mangled bone covered with unsightly scar tissue, which made all the nurses tear up every time they washed me. So after four weeks, my unsightly stump and I were discharged as the nurses grimaced, knowing full well the unspoken difficulties that lay ahead of me. When I got home, the reality of what really happened almost destroyed me; I was unable to cope with any of it. My uncontrollable crying fits were spent in the locked bathroom where my rage and pain battled it out. Binging on prescribed morphine, I waited for the hideous pain to subside.

"But how did you ...?" whispered Sara.

"No, let me go on," I said. "The doctors apparently weren't too concerned about my becoming addicted to the stuff since they gave me bottles of it, but it quickly happened. One day while peering into the mirror, I despised what looked back at me. Crying my last tear, I suddenly dumped numerous bottles of pain medicine down the unsuspecting toilet, watched as they whirled around and around being sucked into its vortex. Vowing never to take another morphine tablet, I quit cold turkey, just like that. My self-pity had made me sicker than I ever was. Forcing myself beyond the pain, I saw a legless man, but not a helpless one. Convincing myself of this, I managed with what remained. Yet, as weeks followed days, it proved too much for me to follow my best intentions, so my anger took over, suffocating me.

"But why didn't you try and see someone, a counselor, to talk out what you were going through?" Sara asked, wanting so much to say something that mattered.

"Well, remember back then, thirty-five years ago, there were no counselors to counsel, only family, and that was thought to be enough, but it wasn't," I replied, remembering how desperately I had needed someone to talk to besides the significant seven, my family. Instead of facing things, I buried them, mostly in Jerri, my steady girl, who before I knew it, became my wife. For a while things seemed hopeful. I was making me into us, although it was cramped quarters living with Mama, Papa, and my remaining brothers and sisters who hadn't yet departed on their life journeys."

"But how did you manage with so little privacy, with so many people?" said Sara, being very glad she didn't have to re-live that particular part when she became the second Mrs.

"Privacy was the last thing on my mind, considering that I had been bathed by total strangers for a month at the hospital, so I guess that part wasn't an issue with me," I said. "My family was my clinging comfort, and being married to Jerri didn't change anything. I could have done without their well-meaning pity, which only compounded my feelings of inadequacy. The thin, tattered walls didn't protect their guarded whispers: the brother whom they had relied on for just about everything had vanished. Each one of them was torn apart because now I was helpless, angry, and out of control, so unlike the old me, the me they had adored, coveted, and depended on. It was unbearable to face their wide-eyed stares, full of defiance, refusing to accept the reality that their two-legged handsome brother had been taken from them without their consent. The shock was just too much for them; it was as though they had lost a leg instead of me. I was the one who should have been screaming out loud in their faces instead of watching frightened eyes and overhearing frantic conversations. To make matters worse, Mama and Papa were terrified that my doting pregnant older sister, Aylvia, would lose her baby if she found out about the accident. They just refused to let her see me. But Aylvia, being Aylvia, just arrived one day after hearing too many excuses. She and her very pregnant belly took one look at me, fainted, and hit the floor, sending everyone into a tail spin.

"Was Aylvia all right? Was the baby?" asked Sara, unable to even imagine the scenario that her distraught husband had just described.

"Yes, Aylvia and her daughter-to-be were fine, but there was someone who wasn't, and that was Mama," I said. "When I came home from the hospital, she was never the same; I thought maybe it was my relationship with Jerri, but it wasn't. Crying continuously, Mama just couldn't seem to accept what had been taken from me ... my leg and my future. It was as though she disappeared into a trance, gave up, didn't care, and cried and cried and cried like a saturating downpour of a tropical monsoon. Because of her constant crying, she somehow damaged the optic nerve in her right eye and became permanently blind in that same eye. Not really wanting to see, Mama's subconscious mind partly granted her that wish, and nothing was ever the same after that. To make matters worse, Jerri and Mama had never really seen eye to eye, even with two eyes, so now it was doubly hard for Jerri to relate to Mama. Actually, I don't know what bothered Mama about Jerri the most, whether it was her age, her lack of education, her family, or her barrio ways. Mama had always envisioned my marriage to a professional somebody, someone who had made it, not a mere schoolgirl who had definitely come from a troubled background and made some wrong choices."

"You know sometimes it is hard for mothers to accept anyone who loves their son, right background or not," Sara butted in. "It is just so unnerving for them to have to share. Especially in your situation, when so much of you had been taken from your Mama already, so suddenly, so horribly," said Sara, feeling stuck between Jerri and Mama.

Because she had heard about several of my childhood experiences and their consequences, Sara was secretly relieved that she never had to endure Mama's scrutiny. Mama passed away six months before she met me.

"Was Jerri able to persevere despite all that was going on around her?"

"Yes, at first, but then I watched Jerri quietly unravel like a strand of colored yarn on a favorite, worn-out sweater," I replied. "She was just a kid herself, all of eighteen, and only knew me as I was prior to the accident: a doer, someone who was involved, patient, so unlike the angry, selfish man that I became. When you added the dagger looks from Mama, I guess it was just too much. So seeking comfort elsewhere, Jerri began to wander, but I remained steadfast because I had two, beautiful brown eyes that were always fixated on me, not knowing that dads were made without crutches."

"The eyes belonged to your daughter, Michelle?" asked Sara, knowing that they were. She had experienced firsthand the inflexible bond that existed between them, recalling how hard it was for Michelle to accept her after having her Daddy all to herself for eighteen years. "How did you ever manage with Michelle if Jerri wasn't there to help you?" queried Sara, trying to sound out the unspoken pieces.

"It wasn't easy, and you know I wasn't really ever sure I could take care of her until that one defining day. Carrying Michelle in my arms, who must have been nearly one at the time, I slipped on the kitchen floor almost dropping her. But I held on for dear life, refusing to let go and somehow protected her in falling when I hit the floor. A blood-curdling scream filled my ears, but it wasn't Michele's. It was Mama's. Witnessing the fall, Mama rushed in to rescue Michelle, but Michelle wouldn't budge. It was amazing. All she said was "No," so I did, too. Keeping Mama at an arm's length, I pulled myself over to the counter and edged myself up with Michelle still snuggled in my arms. As I went from knee to leg to foot, I realized that I could do it by myself and stood up. I guess Michelle knew it all along but needed me to know it. So from then on I wasn't afraid of falling. I wasn't afraid of anything."

"I guess Mama was just trying to shield you from any other setback, knowing full well that you had already had more than your fair share," said

Sara, wondering how Polo had survived with only one leg while negotiating with two well-meaning women and an inspiring daughter.

"Thinking back, the only real setback was waiting, waiting for it. The doctors were so skeptical themselves, always hemming and hawing since they didn't know when and if I would be ready for it. The numerous attempts at re-shaping my stump were ongoing because the doctors were determined to get it right enough so that I could be fitted with a prosthesis. I had pretty much given up on the remote possibility, but I felt Michelle deserved to know that trousers were made for two legs instead of one. That one obsessed thought kept me going. After about a year and a half of uncertainty, the sought-after day finally arrived when I was fitted with a heavy, wooden prosthesis that seemed to drag me behind it. Prosthesis or not, the doctors then informed me that I would always need crutches. Determined to prove them wrong, I threw away the crutches within six weeks and used a crude cane instead. With sheer madness I then refused to use the cane and walked, fell, walked, and fell some more. Within time with my real leg encouraging the fake one, my gait developed, and I stopped falling as much. It was as though a latch was loosened and I was partly freed, knowing I was no longer the Barrio's prisoner. Finishing my last semester of rudely-ignored pharmacy classes was now an option."

"You mean you went back to the University of Houston?" questioned Sara, wondering if that had even been a remote possibility at the time.

"No, that was out of the question, but what ended up as the nearest possibility was the University of Texas Pan American in Edinburgh, which was only fifteen minutes away from the house," I replied. "Venturing out slowly, I fumbled, stumbled, and fell. Taking only a few classes per semester, I finished up knowing that I still had the sharpest mind around. The accident hadn't touched my determination, only strengthened it. Choices, it's all about choices. The twenty-year-old drunk driver who took my leg made some wrong choices. But I had a choice to make as well—to survive. Legless was a different kind of fight, and I fought to make it through every single day. Fighting exhaustion, I had to develop my stamina because it just wasn't there. The pain remained nameless, but it remained, getting more defiant as I got older. Now, I just don't know how much more I can take ... it doesn't involve you or us; it just is more than I can bear."

With that said I curled on my side while Sara untangled the well-used heating pad, placing it on my stump, frantically searching for the big pink pills, the pain deadeners. Muffling her tears, she knew how much agony her husband was in and felt helpless. She thought his recent heart surgery had been the crippler. It wasn't. His heart had been fixed. But this, Sara couldn't fix this. She didn't know how.

THE OUTHOUSE

At one hundred and fifty dollars an hour, I was frustrated, waiting for my scheduled appointment. The longer I waited for Doctor Franco, the shrink, the angrier I got. Then as his sterile, brown eyes penetrated mine, I felt vulnerable and disgusted with myself, not being accustomed to such intense scrutiny. It was as though I were a ripened avocado being prodded and poked to determine if it were ready for sale.

"Tell me, Doctor Saenz, why are you so angry?" questioned Doctor Franco as he peered at me through his impenetrable brown-tinted contact lenses. On his nearly bare desktop was a ticking gold watch. Twiddling his pencil in semi-circled patterns, he checked his timepiece often, as though reassuring himself that I had only so many minutes to reach a conclusion. "Do you still feel frightened because of your recent quintuple bypass heart surgery that you have just undergone, or is it your troubling stump?"

"Do you think that I feel frightened?" I angrily replied. "I have never been frightened by anyone or anything, not even a bully. As a young boy ..." I stopped, making a fist, as though I had to defend myself.

"Tell me about being a young boy," said the doctor, who now appeared somewhat more interested, shifting his upper body so that it was directly in front of my face. Once again I was that seven-year-old boy clinging to fear ... remembering ...

The room was so still that I could hear the wind whistling through the cracks in the wall. With no hesitation I flung myself out of bed onto the cold hard dirt floor, ready to face my greatest fear: myself. "Can I do it?" I wondered out loud. "Can I actually handle the terror of the night alone, without my brother's hand to clutch?" I began to breathe slowly, in and out, watching my heart pound in my chest, thinking it might just burst. It couldn't, I convinced myself, at least not until I had thought through my plan. It was simple enough, although the more I thought about it, the more complicated it seemed. A chilly draft of air ruffled the makeshift curtain that hung limply by the windowsill, allowing me to catch a glimpse of the 'shed.' There, I said it. Actually it was an outhouse that we had renamed for prying visitors who always questioned what it was. You see, I was very much a part of a very proud, although very poor, family. We had to do the best we could with what we had, and I didn't mind because I didn't know that there was any other way. As my thoughts wandered in and out, I stretched out my quivering hand, cautiously reaching for the familiar doorknob that would lead me to answers that lay deep inside myself. With one unwilling step in front of the other, I watched my feet carry me past the peeling paint on the weathered door. As I glanced back, I wondered why I had never noticed the different hues of color that stubbornly remained on the worn-out door. Flickering fireflies darted back and forth on the path like lights on an airplane's runway while the moonlight cascaded across the silvery branches of my favorite well-climbed ash tree.

Suddenly the sweetness, the tenderness of Mama's voice filled my ears. "You are my little soldier."

That thought, that sound pounded in my ears. She truly believed that I could do anything, but this; would she expect me to face the shadows of the night alone? "Yes, of course," I replied out loud, unaware that I had reached the shed. Shrinking against its rough surface, I realized that I had won the outhouse battle, disregarding the need to use it or not. An unaccustomed calmness overtook me as I curiously gazed at the many wondrous shapes that were all around me. Everything was so different at night. There was a certain stillness, a creeping sense of illusion because things were not what they seemed. Startled by a shrill trill of a mockingbird, I clamored hastily back up the beaten path, slipping back into my bed, well, 'our bed,' into my coveted spot, which came at the end of an assortment of heads and toes belonging to my other brothers and sisters.

"So, I hear you saying that you had other battles? What about?" interjected Doctor Franco, who was listening intently.

I answered, "Growing up," and went on ...

"Pato, Pato," I heard someone yell persistently from across the room. How I disliked that nickname given to me at a young age by my father because I waddled like a cute little duck. Can you imagine being called a duck for the rest of your life? I couldn't. I blew a bit of air in front of my face and watched it swirl in wisps and disappear; it was unseasonably cold for this time of year. As I glanced under my feet, the frigid clumps of dirt reminded me to put on both pairs of my thin-worn socks before putting on my new shoes that I had just inherited from my brother. Suddenly I recalled what happened to me last night, and I wanted more than anything to share it with my older brother, Samuel. You see, everyone looked up to Samuel and expected him to do the unexpected; however, this time I was the one who would cause eyes to widen and mouths to quiver. Hurriedly, I headed toward the warmth of the kitchen, but early morning sounds were deafened by a commotion coming from Mama, who instantly could alter my feelings. Now I was on edge.

"Samuel, how many times have I told you to be more careful with the few things that we have?" queried Mama. "How could you possibly have dropped the milk pitcher; don't you realize that that milk had to last us for the rest of the week?"

Samuel didn't bother to answer yet hung his head in dejection. Samuel wasn't awfully sure of anything, and now was no exception. As Mama glared at the milk-soaked boards, I tried to salvage some before our cat, Snoops, eyeing the rare treat, beat me to it. I never could figure out why Samuel always fell apart so easily, so unlike the way I logically reacted.

Mama never waited for anyone to regain their composure, and as if on cue she slowly began to leaf through her worn, tireless companion, her Bible. It was a steadfast tradition at our house that before breakfast the entire family would pray, giving thanks for our existence, however humble it was. The rest of the family had scurried into view by this time, and we all locked hands. Papa's observant eyes were darting back and forth from one to another, waiting for silence to take hold. Smiling inside, I knew that my papa was just as anxious as the rest of us to get on with our day. On this particular day, I lifted up my bowed head, peeping around at the close-knit circle of embraced hands. Feeling an overwhelming warmth, I was drenched in love, determined to keep this closeness no matter what might happen or what might try to divide us. Little did I know at the time that it really would be up to me to prevent this feeling from fading away.

"And have you kept your family together, I mean this closeness that you speak of?" queried the good doctor, fastening his eyes on my tightened fists.

"Let me continue. I can't keep re-directing my thoughts," I said as I relaxed my fists a bit, whirling back into time.

After the morning ritual, Papa pulled me aside.

"Pato, how would you like to help me fix the car's engine? It is sputtering oil again." Papa hoped that I would say yes, but the thought of getting my hands soaked in oil and grease made me shudder. That smell, it was enough to make anyone lightheaded. Today I needed to be alert because it was Saturday, my library day.

Papa wanted to be sure that I was into manly things as well as books. I chirped, "Papa, maybe tomorrow, but today, well, you know it's ..." I didn't need to finish, because he just gave me one of those confused looks. He usually had no use for books, especially on a Saturday.

A warm spicy aroma of beans and eggs filled the air, so my nose led the way. If I didn't get there when the food was ready, there wouldn't be any. My sisters had a prideful gleam in their eyes when I sat down to eat. Not wanting to be embarrassed with a growling stomach, I quickly ate then hurried toward the library where I was allowed to lose myself in other people's lives.

"I'm hearing that books have always been a part of your life," said Doctor Franco and paused, awaiting a response from me. I just continued as though I were trudging onward, seeing my shadow beside me.

As I walked down the dusty dirt road, I glanced about, seeing what I always saw: small tattered shacks dotted with tiny windows that begged to be painted. From the windows, tired, weathered faces happily peered out at me. Children's calls beckoned to one another as if a secret code were known by all. Just then there was an unusual blast of cold wind out of the north that the natives called a Norther, and I began to shiver. Every palm tree was swaying violently in unison like a practiced war dance. Straight ahead were columns of reddish bricks, which surrounded a small brick building that stood ready and willing to allow my entrance into another world. When I opened the door, it always squeaked; how amazing that such a quiet place could have such a noisy door. A sudden gush of warmth overtook me inside and out. Heat, I felt heat, a luxury that we couldn't afford at home. Warming up, I began to focus on other things: the high ceilings with trance-like multi-faceted lights. You could really see what you were looking for and actually read all of it. At home there were a few dimly-lit lamps but little opportunity to get close to them. Then I was jarred out of my thoughts.

"Polo, how nice to see you again," greeted Mrs. Torres, the librarian. It was so good to hear my real name instead of Pato. I loved the sound of my name; it was like music to my ears.

"Mrs. Torres seemed connected to you somehow; did you stay in contact with her as years went by?" interrupted Dr. Franco, speaking rather abruptly, as though he were piecing together a mind puzzle, focusing on the missing parts. "Does she know that you became a professor? She would probably be so proud of you, knowing that you did something with your books that you so loved."

"I don't care if people know whether I'm a professor or not; I never use my title, never have and never will. Did you know that? It is very pretentious and assuming, and I am neither of these things, and in answering your question, I have no idea what happened to Mrs. Torres; it was another lifetime," I answered, still wanting to return to that lifetime ... remembering ...

"Mrs. Torres, have the books come in?"

Anxiously waiting for her reply, I gazed silently at her knowledgeable ways, trying to be patient. I eyed her closely as she scurried to the back of the library, returning with her arms full of Abraham Lincoln and other books. Presidents always fascinated me because many of them had struggled growing up, knowing the rawness of poverty as I did, which made them stronger, more resilient. This gave me hope, realizing that although you couldn't change how and why you were brought into this life, you could change what you did with your life. This was the thread that bound my character together.

Not only was Mrs. Torres the holder of books; she also was instrumental in helping me see how numbers helped you locate corresponding material in an organized fashion. It started with the index cards and quickly became a game of speed after I mastered the ability to memorize countless rows of book numbers. This sparked my love of research.

Biographies were often handed to me, but the poets, especially the Mexican poets, were much more difficult to find. The game got harder since the poets' writings were often housed within other poetry books. Right now I was extremely intent on finding the Mexican poet Juseo Sierra. Adoring Mexican poetry was largely due to my dear Mama, who introduced me to the genre when I was about five years old. Begging her to read the lines over and over, I found that I could hear and remember them. Wanting to show me off to the neighbors, Mama set up my daily performances on our well-used porch accompanied with our well-worn stools. At about five o'clock, the words tumbled out of my mouth, and I became the poet. As I lamented about love, family, and other poetic secrets, tears of compassion and sentiment would roll down the sunken cheeks of the women, while the men shuffled their feet uncomfortably, partly closing their eyes, remembering heart tugs from their pasts. When the performance ended, nickels were thrown toward me, shimmering in the last rays of daylight as they fell around my feet. It was important for these faces to hear and see something beautiful even if only for a moment.

"You like performing, don't you?" asked Doctor Franco, who was insistent that I at least answer one of his pointed questions; however, I didn't and felt as though I were still searching for Sierra.

"Within a matter of minutes, three to be exact, Sierra's poetry was grasped tightly in my grip. What a record, I thought and smirked. Maybe Mrs. Torres would hire me as an assistant; then I could start saving for my dream: college, which seemed unattainable since no one in my family from past or present generations had been able to attend.

"Automatically heading down to the reading table, I noticed an older girl glancing in my direction. She gave me a long look, the kind that makes you want to hold your breath. Were all the buttons on my shirt buttoned the right way, and was my hair going in the right direction? Did she think that I looked smart or funny? While I was trying to figure all this out, I realized the long look was meant for an older boy who was behind me; however, when I passed she winked at me. Grinning, I knew that was good enough. My books were waiting."

"Times up," I heard the doctor announce as he carefully put down his pen, cleared his voice, and paused, waiting for me to say something meaningful.

I did. After I left.

THE DIRGE

"**Y**our time is up, not mine," I muttered, feeling indignation swell inside me like a balloon eager to get off the ground and soar. Adjusting my rearview mirror, I mimicked Doctor Franco, "Times up," and cursed. "My time is definitely not up, not by a long shot," I shouted wildly, wanting the whole world to hear. "Now I do have time, not like before when all I heard was the hemming and hawing of heart surgeons as they decided whether or not they would be able to perform my life-threatening heart surgery: de-clogging five vital arteries at once while creating new ones from veins in my legs ... remembering ...

"We can't possibly do it right away; we just don't have an available operating room or surgeons; the waiting list ..." Doctor Assume chillingly stopped as my mouth dropped a few inches, not believing what I was hearing: "the waiting list?" I couldn't hold on much longer; knowing that it had to be now at this hospital, traveling or postponing was out of the question. I would never make it.

Listening to the no's made me shrink inside as another white-coat scurried in.

"We have a cancellation, five o'clock in the morning for OR. I have assembled a team of four doctors who are willing to do the surgery, although it will be somewhat complicated and long. Not to worry because these doctors are the finest heart surgeons in the Valley; their reputation precedes them," said Doctor Surein, who was wrapped in a spotless white coat.

My shrinking stopped. "It is a go," I repeated, seeing wings fluttering all around this reassuring doctor as Sara, her parents, my sisters, and daughter huddled around my bedside like football players waiting for the play. Although now the star quarterback was no longer needed, as the strategy was being dictated from above, so I closed my heavy eyes, thanking my powerful God for intervening, then sleep captured my torn-up soul.

Hours passed. I opened my eyes but wished that I hadn't. Feeling off balance, I was tugged one way then another by my emotions. I would make it. Could I make it? What if I didn't make it? Sara just stared at me as if I were a ghost. Then her eyes weakened, looking very scared.

"You know, it is going to be all right," I heard myself say, yet I was unconvinced at the sound of the words. I knew that if I presented some type of clarity, Sara would probably trust my instinct and calm down. My poor "wifey," as I affectionately called her since the term wife seemed so abrasive. It was too much, too soon, all in such a short time. We had only been married three years, still newlyweds, still figuring each other out. Academia and free-flowing creativity do not always see things in the same way, especially when flexibility was not a word in either of our vocabularies. But our souls were so bound together that major differences faded, we needed each other ... now this.

Sara started rattling a hundred miles an hour. "Three nights ago when I came home late, really late, because of my student council outing, I was confused and very concerned since you were nowhere to be found. There were no notes, no messages, just the lounging indentation of your lower torso on the empty sofa's cushions. Feeling certain that you had been in an accident and were lying in a gutter somewhere without your cell phone, I decided to search for you along your daily college route. Waiting was not an option. At that instant the phone shrieked wildly, demanding attention. It was Michelle telling me that you were at the hospital, the emergency room and ... all I heard was emergency room. Dropping the phone, I raced to that over-stuffed building with its clinical air, jammed myself in its helpful elevators, scurried down its numerous hospital wings with their commotion-filled hallways, and finally found you. Then I could function. But this is different; nothing is certain. I can't find you. I can't help you. I don't know how ..." Burying her face in my hospital gown, she wept uncontrollably.

With longer intervals between her sobs, Sara slowly whispered, "Three days ago I was sure that you just had one of your non-stop splitting migraines or a severe case of physical exhaustion. I thought that you only needed rest, and I was anxious to get you home. Thank goodness you didn't listen to me, the doctors, or the test results but stubbornly insisted on staying right where you were."

Sensing I needed to take control I said, "Sara, do you remember how terrified you were three years ago at the altar, choking on your 'I do?' You trusted me, held my hands, peered deeply into my eyes, and heard me say calmly, 'I do' without choking. We were not sure what to expect, only sure that God would take care of our love, and He always has. Sara, nothing has changed, but now God is completely in charge. Yes, for once in my life I was selfish, when I insisted on staying at the hospital. Maybe it wasn't the first time," I softly said, trying to get her to raise the corners of her mouth. "My inner voice insisted that there was something very wrong, so leaving the hospital was not an option. Now, at least I know what is wrong and that there is a very high expected survival rate for this intricate type of surgery." Oh, why did I have to say it that way? The statistics didn't need to be voiced; she never was a number person, nor did she see the necessity to be. Lifting her chin, I stumbled on, "Sara, I don't know what is going to happen, but I do know that now you need to be strong for me because I can't worry about you, Michelle, or anyone else. It has to be another one of those selfish times. All my energy and thoughts need to be positive, no what ifs, or I will never be able to endure what is twelve hours away. Do you think you can do that for me?"

Without missing a beat, Sara wiped away her last tear, at least the last one that her husband would see.

Later that evening while I dozed on and off, soft murmurs woke me from unconsciousness, my retreat. As I reluctantly opened my eyes, a kind face encircled by a white collar came into view.

"Dr. Saenz," I heard the face sincerely ask, "may I pray with you?"

At the time I couldn't think of anything that I needed or wanted more. Well, maybe ... just the certainty that I would survive the next twenty-four hours. If anyone could give me some sort of answer, this encircled face probably could.

"You know, Reverend, there are so many ifs right now; I'm just not sure whether I can do what everyone expects me to do in six hours." There, I finally said it. Maybe I should just say my goodbyes now and be done with it."

"Being confused is perfectly normal," the reverend quietly said. "After all, this has been so unexpected, so unnatural for you. Being a professor you are accustomed to being in control, being the last one to leave the college's parking lot, and now you are worrying that you aren't going to get the semester grades turned in on time."

What, did he really just hear what I was thinking? How did he know all of that? Feeling jolted, I reached down beside me, feeling the soft leather cover of my incomplete grade book with its embossed UTB emblem. Half-graded term papers were tossed every which way on the bed sheets, adding to the Reverend's psychic ability. Maybe he couldn't read minds after all, but his view seemed clearer than most. Then it sank in. Who else would be working on grades at a time like this except for a dedicated professor, a responsible professor, a lost professor? Free-flowing tears scattered themselves down my face.

"My students need their grades; they are due," I said, knowing that I just couldn't stop.

"Dr. Saenz, your students will survive if their grades are incomplete; all that is important now is that you are complete," replied the kind reverend, reaching for my trembling hands that were not used to being out of control. "Worry and doubt never allow healing, but trust in our Lord and Savior will. All you need to do is ask."

"I don't know that I am worthy of asking," I said, feeling like a bowl full of chilled jello.

The minister hesitated, knowing that he could reach me and wasn't going to give up.

"Is that your significant other outside with the curly dark hair and unnerving brown eyes?"

"Well, yes, one of them. My daughter, Michelle, I am all that she has, she ..." I stopped, cringing, knowing the panic that she must be wading in. In my mind's eye, I could just see her frantically pacing up and down the hallways, trying to figure out how to "fix it." Armed with her cell phone and determination, she probably had contacted every available resource center hoping to learn about all the ins and outs of this edgy operation. Michelle was so much like me, self-reliant, outgoing yet fearful, and she, too, didn't know how to ask. "Equally significant but in a very different way is my devoted wife, Sara, who unlike Michelle is quiet, reserved, but does know how to ask. I am certain that is all she has been doing since leaving this room a short while ago. She depends so much on me; I am her only friend, her best friend, and she never lets me forget that honorable fact. I don't think it's very healthy to rely on just one person for interaction. I mean, she loves to talk to me, and talk and talk and talk. I can't imagine what would happen to her if my ears weren't there to hear her."

"Are there others who need you, love you, and are incomplete without you?" asked the reverend.

"Many, too many," I said, sensing where he was going with this conversation.

"May I call you Polo?" questioned the reverend, bowing his head, closing his eyes, and waiting to see if I did also. He didn't need to wait. It happened naturally as my fingers clasped themselves. "Lord, our merciful Father, give Polo the strength," started the reverend, and then we prayed and prayed some more. Afterwards I felt a tremendous rush of hope race through every pore in my body; the doubt had vanished like an early morning fog on a chilly day and was replaced with an odd sensation of penetrating peace. Then and only then did I know that I was going to make it, six, eight, ten hours, whatever it took, because I was no longer afraid. He was with me ... and I slept.

However, my peaceful slumber was rudely interrupted when a middle-aged, stocky lady clad in a white uniform with cap grunted a greeting of sorts and started wielding her mechanical arms, shaving my very noticeable hairless chest with non-stopping gusto. After some obsessive shaving, she assured me that it was all a part of pre-operation protocol. Yes, I thought, but whose? My audience's eyes hardly moved as they watched sleepily since they had both slept on the floor by my bed in rolled blankets that the night nurse had provided. Evidently blankets were very scarce items that were closely monitored, but Michelle and Sara weren't leaving, and tile floors get pretty cold. Thank goodness the night nurse was more nurturing than this one.

A young, well-built orderly pounced through the doorway, so much energy, so early; it was only 4:00 a.m.! What do they feed their employees? I need to get some of it. I made a mental note. By this time the drugs had definitely taken their effect as I was hoisted on the wheeled guerney and escorted down the barren hall. Seven pairs of hands tightly gripped the silver-coated side railings. My two significant others had been joined by my five doting sisters, who had just arrived in time for the procession. As I looked groggily around, it was rather like a funeral march: drawn faces were distorted in fear while red-streaked eyes stared ahead, not focusing. All that I wanted to do at that moment was to jump up and assure everyone that they would indeed see me again in ten hours, breathing. As I waited for the dirge to start, we suddenly arrived at our destination, a small room outside the operating room, rather like a holding pen where countless patients were shivering in their drug-induced stupors while their loved ones lost all control. My slot was selected, blankets were piled on top of me, and Sara was allowed to linger, looking at me as though through a camera's lens, memorizing every flawed though handsome feature on my pale face.

She then gushed like a drenching downpour, "I know who you are and what you stand for. You have always loved me the way I am, even though I hate cooking," she stated with a frozen face. "I don't think that I have ever thanked you for putting up with me, for giving me confidence, and for allowing me to change at my own dictated pace. Polo, oh, my loving Polo, I just can't lose you; we have only just started our journey; there is just too much that waits for us. I ..." Then she lost control and smothered me with permanent kisses as her eyes darted around like a terrified baby bird that had just tumbled out of its cozy nest. Now we were forced to part, so much tenderness, so little time. Trying to soothe her, I caressed her cold fingers, and then weakly smiling at her, I gave her a permanent kiss of my own. Her darting eyes had suddenly spotted someone, someone she had to talk to, someone who could make all the difference. Strategically making her way toward my surgeon, she opened her sinking soul. Watching her lips move while her eyes cried, I guess she was trying to convince the doctor that she really loved me, hoping that he would do his best, take his time, and allow her to see me again alive; I guess she convinced him. Being very heavy, my eyes had seen enough drama and closed.

As I was escorted into the operating room, Sara, her parents, Michelle, my five sisters, and my youngest brother, Tito, were escorted up to the waiting room, a room where fears were faced and conversations were left unfinished. When the operation got under way, only one person was permitted phone contact with the surgeon, and that unwanted honor went to Sara, who hated the telephone, especially now when countless ears strained for any spoken clue.

Dreading every ring, Sara debated whether or not to answer, yet each call ended a three-hour torment. Between rings Sara's mind persuaded her to leave, to run away, but every beat of her healthy heart convinced her to stay. So she listened to meaningless sounds, sipped crank-oil coffee, and held her mother's soft, reassuring hand. After the second ring, a group prayer was organized by Brad, their pastor, whom Sara had called earlier for spiritual backup. Brad was very calm, concentrating on the power of prayer instead of uncertainty. Insisting that they all clasp hands, he asked God for His intercession and mercy, praying the way only a minister can pray. Then he, too, sipped tasteless black coffee. The room looked like a scene from an old-time silent movie. Polo's immediate family glued themselves together on one side of the room, while Sara and her parents strayed to the other side. His sisters were sitting exactly the same way, left leg over right, in a straight, confining row like pegs on a piece of wood. Their heads bowed into the daily paper, losing themselves in the produce ads. It was as though the ads somehow guaranteed that there would be a tomorrow. Tito, who was a successful director of a federal housing agency, positioned himself at the end of the line, immersed in continuous paperwork as his recently buffed leather loafers screamed of rank. Michelle, stationed beside Tito, popped up every few minutes, hanging onto her cell phone as if it were a life preserver.

Sara's parents seemed equally as fascinated with the ads, not taking their eyes off them. What was it about the newspaper during a crisis? Sara refused even to pick up one section of it. What did any of it really matter if she lost her much-loved husband? The commanding wall clock and she had become inseparable. Her eyes never left its face. With time, eyes reddened and spirits deflated like slow-leaking tires. It was four o'clock. The phone rang for the last time. Nine hours had passed since their loving brother, much-loved son-in-law, adoring father, and nurturing husband had been wheeled away to the dreaded operating room. Sara gazed at her parents, wishing that she could disappear forever, not wanting to know, terrified of what the voice had to say on the other end of the phone. Chills raced through her entire body as every eye in the room saturated her with doubt.

Grasping the handle of the cold plastic phone, she carefully lifted it up to her ear, and the voice said, "He made it and is on his way to the recovery room."

She wept tears of thankfulness. When she turned around, arms were tangled and cheeks were wet. Their powerful God had granted their bequest, and Polo had been spared.

Meanwhile, slowly waking up in the recovery room, I heard the nurse gently say, "Put this back in your mouth. You will be needing it." It was my partial plate. I knew then that I had made it. They trusted me with my own teeth. God had given me a second chance, and I took it.

DELAWARE PUNCH

As the wings of time slowly brought me back to the present, I realized that I was weaving back and forth on the road in my SUV. I was experiencing one of my unwanted, unnerving panic attacks. I couldn't breathe. My heart pounded with tremendous force, and the dizziness created a murky film, camouflaging everything around me. From deep inside I heard a murmur rising to the surface.

"Don't fight it, don't fight it, just go with it, breathe slowly, deeply, calmly."

So for once, I listened. My chest stopped heaving, and my nose started breathing. But by the time it ended, my throat felt like a parched, cracked driveway. I needed something to drink––something cold, something soothing.

Finding the closest convenience store, I bought and inhaled the cold, syrupy, sweet reddish liquid better known as a Delaware Punch, recalling many times as a boy when I would go miles out of my way after visiting the library just to drink a whole bottle without having to share.

Quietly gathering up my books, I headed for the squeaky door of the library.

"Polo, don't stay up too late reading your books," whispered Mrs. Torres, smiling from ear to ear.

Even if I wanted to, it would be impossible with the crowded conditions at my house, I thought. But this was my second house, a house of learning where there was plenty of room, light, and a smiling lady who whispered and knew my real name.

I turned abruptly at the corner of South St. and trudged toward Woolworth's little swinging sign, which was trying its best to resist the blowing wind. It was the end of a near-perfect day. However, as I turned the knob and heard the little bell rattle, I regretted my thirst and wished I had never heard of a Delaware Punch.

"Well, look who's here. If it isn't little Pato." The words jumped out at me. I looked around and saw what no eleven-year-old boy wanted to see when he was by himself: one of the bullies of the neighborhood, grinning from ear to ear.

I was small for my age, although at that moment I think I got smaller losing a few more inches from sheer terror. I made myself stand up very tall and threw my shoulders back, yet I was still miles below his shoulders.

I made a noise come out of my mouth, and it went something like this: "Jose, what do you want?"

"Don't you know that this is my favorite store and that no one comes in here unless I say that they can?" he jeered at me.

"No, I didn't know those were the rules for admittance. When did they go into effect?" I swallowed hard, not believing that I had actually said that. It must have been someone else who had answered him. Those words couldn't have come out of my mouth, but they did. Jose looked at me in disbelief.

"My, aren't we a little daring for being so far away from home?" he muttered. Suddenly I knew that I had gone too far, but I didn't care.

I darted forward and tried in vain to look for something red in one of the soft-drink containers. It was too late. I felt a hand on my shoulder and waited for the hard punches to start, but they didn't. Instead, a friendly voice asked me, "Is there something I can help you with?"

It was none other than Mr. Martinez, the owner of Woolworth's. I couldn't believe it. Mr. Martinez had saved me and didn't even know it, or did he?

"Delaware Punch, please," I said and gulped.

"Son, they are over here on this side." It was his side. Jose just stood there and glared at me, waiting to close in on me at my most vulnerable moment. It didn't happen. Mr. Martinez stayed quite close to my side until I had a Delaware Punch firmly clutched in hand and was in front of the cash register. He seemed to know that Jose was waiting for me. Mr. Martinez must have read my mind and started the most amazing conversation with me; I didn't hear a word of it. Jose grew impatient and with one turn suddenly left the store. I was speechless. I couldn't believe my good fortune, yet I knew this wasn't over and would be continued on the way to school on Monday. How right I was. Mr. Martinez gave me a reassuring nod as I left. Maybe Mr. Martinez was small for his age when he was eleven and was picked on by older boys in his neighborhood. Perhaps he saw those bullies in Jose and decided it was time he fought back. I'm glad that he did.

All the way home, I kept glancing around me. Around every turn and twist in the road, I expected Jose to block my way, but he never did. It seemed as though it took me five hours to get home instead of my usual good time on a windless day of one-and-a-half hours. Nevertheless I was very grateful when our warm little house peeked out from behind the swaying palms welcoming me. Almost choking, I realized just how close I had come to facing my worst nightmare even though I was wide awake. I made sure that I was awake by pinching myself. My eyes were getting blurry as wetness cascaded down my face. It would never do to have Mama or Papa see me like this. I quickly wiped the tears away, taking many short gasps of air, concentrating on my breathing. Forcing myself to calm down, it became very clear to me once again that I had narrowly escaped my tormentor.

"Have I always had trouble breathing when I came face to face with someone or something unexpectedly that frightened me?" I muttered out loud. Maybe this was a pattern that had always been there. Perhaps I had panic attacks back when I was a boy, yet no one had labeled them as such. This thought gave me a glimpse of peace that I needed to grab onto and not let go of.

I guess I was very quiet at supper. Everyone assumed that I was thinking about the latest book that I had discovered at the library, but I wasn't. As I looked around at the table, I wondered if any of my brothers and sisters had felt fear, real panic. When I was with my family, I could always enjoy the conversation and really listen to just what they had to say. It didn't matter if it was silly or if I had heard it one hundred times before; I still wanted to hear it. In our house I didn't have to worry about who was going to be in the next room, and I felt safe. Away from home everything was completely the opposite. Watching my back and wondering if the figure ahead was friend or foe, I tried to use my wits to make up for what I lacked in size.

"Pato, you don't seem your hungry self. Did you snack on the way home?" asked Papa with concerned eyes. He probably was trying to cover for me because Mama's cooking was her pride and joy. She sometimes got her feelings hurt if your plate wasn't wiped clean. I realized the connection he was after and answered him.

"I stopped at Woolworth's for a Delaware Punch, Papa." I guess I must have winced when I uttered the punch part because Papa gave me the strangest look.

"Did you try a new flavor, or was the strawberry not to your liking this time?"

"It wasn't the punch, Papa. It's what happened when I was getting the punch. Actually I almost got punched. Can you believe it? This big guy who bullies everyone thought that I was in his way."

My sister Amberina piped in, "Well, did you run and get help?"

A typical solution for a girl, I thought. Girls always thought you could solve everything by getting help.

"Amberina, it just so happened that help came to me, and I didn't even ask for it. How is that for a story, and it is true; that's exactly what happened." I quickly finished the entire scenario, and my family just looked at me.

"Pato, you know we want you to stay out of trouble, don't you?" queried Mama.

"Yes," but I knew I meant no. I had made up my mind that on Monday I was going to face Jose, not run, not back down, but face him no matter what, no matter what he did to me. I felt a bit better now that I had shared the events of the day with my family, but as I looked around, I saw a lot of worried looks and quiet eyes glancing down at their plates. From that moment on, I decided that I would handle Jose by myself and not cause my brothers or sisters any unneeded worry about what might happen to me.

I quickly diverted the conversation and announced that I had found a book of Juseo Sierra's poetry, and Mama let out a long sigh. A certain longing appeared in her eyes, and I knew that I was out of no-man's-land, saved by the poet, and thoughts were now far away from Jose. I settled in my favorite chair, the one by the lamp, and read until stillness settled in the room. My brothers and sisters entertained themselves with made-up games of hide-and-seek until they were thoroughly exhausted. One by one they clambered into bed as the night wove its star-studded blanket and beckoned me to gaze one more time at its tapestry. Night was such a special time for me, a private time to examine my thoughts without being interrupted by other demanding voices. However, that's not to say that you wouldn't get interrupted by an elbow or two. As I stared at the stars, they seemed to weave a spell over me, assuring me that in the morning everything would be better.

The present, reasserting itself, found me cautiously driving home through the maze of interlocking roads. I prayed for the ability to make it without another episode, a jolting panic attack. My prayers must have had priority because before I knew it, I was wrapped in my wife's loving arms. Then I knew that I was in a safe haven hidden from myself, at least for a while.

THE UNWANTED VISITOR

The steady swelling strength of my wife's heightened voice surged with emotion as she read out loud sections of the Psalms from the Bible, a Sunday ritual that we have kept since the first Sunday of our married life. When my eyes were closed, I could hear my beloved Mama reciting the same exact verses. Sara paused for a moment, studied my face, and quizzically asked, "Polo, what were your Sundays like when you were a boy?" So I told her.

"On Sunday I awoke with a refreshed feeling, and I was eager to start my day. I counted the lumps still in bed, three. I knew Papa would be up. Quietly getting up, I made my way across the room. Papa seemed to know that Sunday was our day; he casually read the paper as he waited for me to join him so that he wouldn't have to finish it alone. Reading was his strong suit, and I knew that he was trying to set an example for me. I loved him for it and followed his example. Unlike me, Papa never had any formal schooling because as a young boy he always had to work. I looked at the headline. My curiosity burst out loud ..."

"Papa, what did the article say about the mayor's race? Who won?" I knew he knew the answer, yet he needed to know if I could figure it out.

"Pato, sit here next to me and read the article out loud, then I will ask you some questions about it. Let's see if you can tell me who won."

Mama said that I learned through his eyes. This made me feel proud, knowing that Papa's eyes were so special.

"Ramirez won and is supposed to help bring water and sewage treatment to colonias like ours. Papa, I bet he will help us out," I insisted.

"Pato, don't you know that only we can help ourselves, solve our own problems? No one really cares how we live, only that we take care of ourselves and do the best that we can with what we have." Papa ruffled my hair and absentmindedly stared straight ahead.

"But I care. I am going to help our people and don't need to be mayor to do it." One thing I would need, though, would be my education, and from that day on, I never forgot that conversation.

I was quickly pulled back.

"Pato, where are your Sunday pants? I ironed them for you, along with your good shirt. Go look for them in your section of the closet," Mama softly directed me. I knew that it wouldn't be too difficult to locate them because, first of all, there weren't that many clothes to choose from. Sunday's best, as Mama called it, was hung neatly on the third hanger, my section. I carefully held my only white shirt that had been freshly pressed up to my face, taking a deep breath of cleanliness and starch, reaching for my one pair of khakis.

"Pato, why do you always take so much time in getting dressed?" asked Amberina, who was also busy getting ready. She got dressed in no time, never being able to figure out why I couldn't.

"Amberina, don't you know that people judge you on your appearance, and it is very important to always look your best? I don't want people at church to feel sorry for me or to pity me. If I look good, they will have good thoughts about me and want to talk to me, not talk about me," I calmly said. Amberina just shrugged her shoulders and said that she had more important things to think about.

"Boys," I thought out loud.

Sunday morning was really quite a scene at our house. With four sisters teasing me, wanting my advice on what to wear, there was never a dull moment, especially when we were preparing for church. We had a ritual on Sunday when Mama would take the girls and Samuel to the Methodist

Church, and Papa and I would depart for the Taylor Institute, my school, which on Sundays served as a non-denominational church where the sermons were literal excerpts from the Bible. I'm not sure how this routine got started, yet it agreed with all of us, especially Papa and me. I loved being alone with my papa and got all the attention I wanted. All I needed was to be near him. Since he worked so much, he was hardly ever home except for Sundays. We were off.

"Pato, how are things going at school?" questioned Papa. I was sitting up in the front of his old fifty, rundown Ford, nudging a bit closer to him.

"You know, Papa, things at school have changed quite a bit this year with my being in sixth grade and all. Everyone sure looks up to me for all the answers and tries to be like me. Remember in second grade that I had never heard of a missionary before?" I quickly searched his face for a gesture.

"Yes, I recall that you were very nervous about going to your school and being taught by missionaries. How do you feel about them now?"

"They are the greatest, Papa. In fact, I don't think I would have enjoyed school as much as I have if I hadn't been taught by them, especially Ms. Gulley. I remember the first time I met Ms. Gulley, who seemed so plain, so simple, and so wonderful. I wondered why she didn't sign her name with a Mrs. or a Miss. Someone told me that she preferred Ms. because she didn't want people to know that she wasn't married. Papa, if I were older, I mean her age, I would have married her in a minute."

Papa turned his head and gave me a look, probably wanting me to explain what I just said, but I kept on going.

"I don't think people should live alone, although at school Ms. Gulley really has all of us as her children. Every day we go to chapel, and without it I would feel very empty inside. Chapel gives me a sense of balance, giving me time to think about what has happened in my day and how I reacted. It calms me." I paused for a moment to collect my thoughts. Papa had turned his head toward me, knowing that I had his undivided attention.

"Pato, how are you getting along with the other boys at school?"

I knew that this was a loaded question, leading somewhere, so I carefully answered.

"Most of the boys are easy to be with, but you know there are a few who just seem to pick on other kids, humiliating them. Did any kids ever bother you, Papa, when you were at school?"

He took a long, deliberate breath, slowly letting it out.

"Times were different back when I was a boy. We went to school to learn, not having the time or energy to get into any trouble." I suddenly noticed that his eyes got misty, and I knew why. His mother had died when he was three. His boyhood was probably much tougher than mine could ever be. I felt empty inside knowing that I made Papa sad. I reached for his hand, which seemed so huge compared to mine, and gave it a loving squeeze.

"Look, we're here," I said quickly, changing the subject. The dome of the chapel glistened with drops of sunlight. The windows contained bits of stained glass: hues of red, purple, and blue that melted together, demanding that you stare at them. I always did and got lost in the colors and shapes.

"Mr. Saenz, Polo, how nice to see you," a low voice said quietly. It was one of my teachers, Mrs. Sanchez. They always seemed so happy to see us in church with our parents. I guess because it reassured them that at least for an hour or two they wouldn't have to monitor our behavior. What a relief for them, I thought.

I quickly searched the pews for a safe haven; it was critical on Sundays not to have any teachers in your pew or even within elbow distance or earshot. The light danced on one of the recently waxed pews, and the wood reflected colors of amber and brown, outlining my face when I glanced into it.

"Papa, let's sit here. We need a quiet place to absorb the sermon without distraction." His eyes met mine, having a distinct twinkle, as if he could read my mind. I closed my eyes, thanking God for my papa and the rest of my family. The smell of lemons wafted through the opened window. For a moment I was in a fragrant garden of gardenias and lemon trees.

Reverend Brown began, "We are happy to see all of you in the house of the Lord." He had a voice like that of a scholar. While I listened I could see God looking at me, knowing that I got into fights, disliked bullies, and sometimes, well, often, wanted my own way. It made me feel funny inside because I sensed that God wasn't too pleased with my performance.

I hoped that he would be busy tomorrow so that he would miss my confrontation with Jose.

Reverend Brown always started the sermon with an excerpt from the Bible, and today was no exception. I reached eagerly in front of me for a Bible that was scrunched in between two hymn books and found the reading passage. When Reverend Brown preached his sermons, I thought that he knew just what I needed to hear to help me through the week, reminding me that God was always there no matter what trouble I happened to find myself in. An old wooden cross hung directly in front of the congregation. It seemed to have a silent power, making you want to change your ways. Gazing at it, I felt very peaceful, determined. Up and down the pews, the ushers passed silver-lined collection plates.

"Papa, get out your envelope; the plate is almost here."

Papa slowly emptied his pocket. Out came a thin white envelope folded neatly in half.

"Pato, place it in the center of the plate so it won't fall out," he said. I peered into his face, seeing a serious look full of pride. I was my father's son. Papa couldn't donate much, but he gave what he could. I carefully placed the donation in the plate and felt a warmth rush over me, knowing that our little gift would help others who might be worse off than we were.

When Reverend Brown finished his sermon, he would always walk down between the pews and gaze at the congregation. As he glanced at me, I wondered what he thought. Did I remind him of his youth, recalling how he also needed a sense of direction from time to time? Once outside the church, Papa and I waited patiently in line to shake the Reverend's hand.

"Pato," I heard an urgent whisper and felt an affectionate nudge. "You look really handsome in your khakis and your tie."

I couldn't believe it; it was Carmen, one of the most beautiful girls from my school. Her blue-green eyes were brimming with smiles. Her easy manner always made me feel warm and wonderful. But I was with my papa; it would never do to get nervous.

"Thank you," I said as calmly as I could, and hoped that would be the end of our conversation. It was. Breathing a silent sigh of relief, I hoped that Carmen understood. Tomorrow I would say something remarkable to her.

"Nice sermon, Reverend Brown," I uttered, always making sure that I shook his hand with a manly grip. Afterwards I knew I had made a special connection with God because of that handshake.

"You and your Papa shared a very special bond that was especially nourished on Sundays. How lucky you were to be able to spend that nurturing time together––just the two of you, sharing the things a boy needs to say only to his father," Sara said, wistfully wishing that she had taken more time to share things with her father when she was a young girl.

"But Sara, things were not always that calm and nurturing on Sundays after church––quite the contrary. Sundays meant visiting hours, people wanting to see Mama and Papa, never knowing when to leave. One Sunday stands out in my mind. It is a day that I will never forget."

The drive home from church seemed very relaxed.

"Pato, do you have studies to prepare for tomorrow?" queried Papa.

"Math and science will take up a few hours, I think." Those two subjects fascinated me. Our old Ford slowly made its way up the dry, cracked clay dotted with sunflower weeds that served as our driveway. If nothing else, our driveway sure had a lot of character.

"Papa, Pato, you're home at last; we've been waiting for you," chimed Aylvia, my older sister. "We just got home ourselves, and Mama is making tortillas." Every Sunday we had a contest to see who would get home first from church. It seemed Aylvia and the rest of my sisters were ahead. Contests livened everything up. We truly loved competing against one another.

"Where's Tina?" I questioned Aylvia. Tina's whereabouts were never far from my mind; I felt a special closeness toward her since I was her protector."

"Pato ..."

I turned and heard a loving mumble from Tina. She grabbed my hand and herded me and Papa into the house. As I watched her help Mama with lunch, I felt in awe of Tina. She never complained about her condition, going out of her way to help all of us. Her condition was a mystery to me, to all of us for that matter. Mama never wanted to discuss it, yet I did manage to wiggle out some information.

"When she was about four years old, Tina saw something or experienced something that terrified her while she was outside the house," Mama told me. "Hearing this terrible shrieking sound, I rushed outside only to find Tina sobbing uncontrollably with a dazed look in her eyes. After bringing her into the house, I thought after a while that she would be her usual talkative self, but she wasn't. Since that day she has spoken very little. When she tries to speak, it is barely audible."

Mama wiped streaming tears from her eyes when she finished, but now at last I had bits of pieces of what happened. From that moment on I vowed to take care of Tina, trying to put the pieces back together in the best way that I could. As the wafting aroma from the tortillas filled the house, strands of silent love knotted us together.

"Pato, would you be able to help me with my addition? I just don't get it," mouthed Avera, her mouth overstuffed with a gigantic tortilla. Avera, who was in second grade, only had to gaze at me with her moonlike hypnotic eyes, which worshiped me. I was hers, and she knew it.

"Sure, addition is simple. Here is a really neat way to help you learn it. Mr. Thomas taught us with toothpicks at school; go ask Mama for some uncooked beans," I replied. I enjoyed showing my sisters how to learn things when they were confused because knowledge came easily to me. I liked how their eyes lit up as they finally figured something out.

The others joined Avera and me on the floor with our beans, and the lesson began.

"Enrique, look at Pato with those kids; he is just like a magnet," I overheard Mama say to Papa. Beaming at me, she gave me that look of hers, one of expectation mingled with pride.

"Hey, that is a good method, and I remember doing something like that an awfully long time ago, too long," piped in my older brother, Samuel, who was watching intently from across the room. Amazing, I thought, for Samuel to acknowledge us, being a high schooler and all. It seemed as though once you were in high school, you developed a phobia against anyone who was below your grade level. When we were visible to Samuel, he became one of us instantly, acting as though he enjoyed us.

"Avera, you must learn your addition very well because when you get to sixth grade much of the math that you do is based on adding numbers together," declared Aylvia, being the little mother that she was, although no one ever listened. A quick rasping knock could be heard on the front door as we all rolled our eyes at one another. If only one Sunday could go by without our being interrupted with pesky visitors. Mama and Papa sure seemed to enjoy them, but why I will never know! Papa readily answered the door while Mama whisked into the kitchen for a plate piled with sweet bread and a quenching pitcher of ice tea.

"Do come in," Papa said warmly to the tall, well-dressed man who clutched a Bible in his left hand. Whenever I saw someone with a Bible in tow, I knew that they probably were connected in some way to the ministry with which Mama was actively involved, spreading the teachings of Jesus Christ to those in or out of jail.

"Good day to all of you on this the Lord's Day," proclaimed Mr. Frank, the visitor, who looked quite out of place with his starched white shirt and choking tie. My mother made Mr. Frank feel welcome, as welcome as a visitor could feel, while Papa made some quick introductions.

"Yes, Marcelina and I are very well acquainted with the good book since Marcelina's father is a Methodist minister." The conversation continued with references made to the Mormons and their beliefs. I tuned out the rambling chit-chat, figuring it was just another Sunday visitor who wanted to share his strong beliefs and question ours. I was very wrong; Mr. Frank not only questioned, but he demanded.

"Surely you can donate some clothing articles that you no longer need and some food items that you can do without," he boldly asserted. Springing up, the words just started tumbling out of my mouth.

"We always do without. We barely have enough to eat; we don't even have enough clothes to wear." I gulped for air and continued, "What gives you the right to come into our house asking for donations when we are the ones who are needy? Why don't you take your own advice and give all that you have to the poor, surviving on your faith?" I suddenly felt the looks, especially the cold stare from Mama.

"Please excuse our son's rudeness," Mama calmly uttered in total embarrassment, but I didn't care. I knew that I had done the unthinkable, but enough was enough. I was tired of people taking advantage of Mama and Papa because of their giving nature. My nature wasn't so giving; if people needed help, let them try at least to help themselves like we had always done. Because of the commotion, Tito, who was asleep, suddenly awoke, screaming the only way a two-year-old can scream. Mr. Frank's neck jerked up and down, looking like he had been captured by his tie. I didn't care. I bolted out the back door while hanging mouths and shocked looks followed me.

Mr. Frank arose just as quickly, as though he had been battered with flying bricks.

"I didn't come to disrupt your Sunday, but it seems that I should leave." And he did abruptly. Out of the mouths of babes he had heard a startling truth.

"I better go and see if I can find Pato," clamored ten-year-old Amberina, the peacemaker in the family. The rest of the family sat motionless, wondering who would break the ice-coated silence that froze them.

"Pato is right. Who helps us when we don't have enough to eat and have to wear the same clothes over and over again? The kids at school think it is our uniform," Aylvia bravely added.

"At school you are clean, neat, and nothing else matters. We do with what we have. That is the end of this conversation," announced a very annoyed Mama, rising and leaving the room. Uncomfortable feelings hung in the air like sleeping bats not wanting to be disturbed.

At about six o'clock that afternoon, there was a creak on a loose floorboard on the front porch as two footsteps crunched slowly toward the door. Mama's sixth sense knew that I had returned to face the music, armed with my convictions. Mama just looked at me; her glance spoke volumes: hurt, pain, disbelief. It was punishment enough. After a few minutes of uncomfortable silence, she grabbed me in a way that made my heart pound and my legs tremble. Feeling a sheer sense of utter relief, I knew that she had forgiven me.

A nourishing dinner of rice and beans with fajitas seemed to calm everyone down, including Papa, who usually let Mama pull in the reins when it came to disciplining our family. Today was no exception. Making no direct eye contact with me, I knew he wasn't at all pleased with my behavior.

"Pato, are Franco and Jesse coming over for our usual Sunday baseball game?" Samuel asked, knowing that a good game outside would help clear the air inside. "I'll get the bat and ball and rummage up something for the bases," rambled Samuel, eager to get outside and direct the game as he always did. I was thankful to escape and get rid of some of my energy, the kind that is half adrenalin and half relief.

"Franco, Jesse, over here," I motioned as I saw the familiar friendly faces of my closest boyhood buddies.

"Pato, you don't look quite right," yelled Jesse, jerking his elbow in my side, trying to make me laugh. I did. There was something about being with your buddies from the barrio that you shared: your poverty and your inability at times to deal with it.

"Boy, are you a sight for sore eyes," Jesse yelped amidst our horseplay, and Franco jumped in right on cue. That night we played baseball as though our lives depended on it, stopping only on Mama's cue when it was time for our nightly Bible reading. Not missing a step, we clamored up the rickety porch stairs for a coveted spot by her familiar well-used rocking chair. The rest of the family was already positioned.

"Tonight we are going to learn about Jacob and his twelve sons. There was a lot of jealousy between the sons, and this is what can happen if you let your emotions get the best of you," continued Mama, thinking this excerpt was perfect for me because of what had happened a few hours ago. Mama read the Bible with such a soft expression yet with such drama. It made you feel that you were there. We were all mesmerized by her voice. She would leave us hanging right in the middle of the verse. No one wanted her to stop, and she knew it. She had acquired this spellbinding technique, and it kindled our love of the Bible.

"You were quite outspoken even as a young boy, weren't you?" asked Sara, who wasn't a bit surprised when she heard of the confrontation with Mr. Frank. As a matter of fact, it sounded exactly like the man she had married. "Were you even a bit fearful of your Mama? What she might do to you?"

"No, even when I was a young boy, I expressed my opinion when I felt that an injustice had occurred. It has always been important to me to right a wrong," I said, thinking about the bully factor and how much of my life it had consumed.

THE BULLY

F acing my first period college class, I scanned the roster. Jose's name screeched out at me in a very irritating way. After all of this time, I couldn't believe that the sight of that name could still bother me so much. But it did. Pieces of my memory jogged together as I recalled how walking to school was very precarious for a twelve-year-old.

"Pato, get up. You went back to sleep," whispered Aylvia softly as she tried to dislodge me from one of my better dreams. "You know that ten minutes is all the time that you have to fully wake yourself up." Since there was only one bathroom and nine of us, including Mama and Papa, bathroom time had to be scheduled.

"Aylvia, how could I make it without you?" I nudged her affectionately.

"You couldn't, not even for a day," she stated matter-of-factly. In a family there are bonds that stand the test of time. We had one. Aylvia was keenly aware of what and how I felt even before I knew it.

"I'm there," I said, swooping toward the dimly lit, tiny hallway leading to the bathroom. The best part about the bathroom was the crack in the mirror. Aside from that there wasn't much space in which to move. But it served us all well, as if it knew it was a necessity in our lives. School mornings were well routined. Each of us was expected to get up, wash, dress, and be ready for morning prayer sharply by 7:00 a.m.

"Avera, put these socks on," I urged my little sister, trying to help her get ready for school. Her reply was indignant. She was bound and determined not to wear the socks.

"No," shouted Avera, "I will dress myself and wear what I please." Oh, to be seven again when you could shout, show your displeasure, and get away with it.

"Pato, how does my hair look this way?" Amberina yanked my shirttail, eagerly searching for my approval, which made me feel good inside.

"Great braids," I replied, wondering if Mama had started the eggs and refried beans wrapped in tortillas. The aroma told me that I had better hurry and get to the table. First come first served in our house.

"Beat you, Pato," Samuel said jeeringly, his fist full of a dripping, bean-stuffed tortilla, ready to be swallowed whole if that were possible. Samuel was somewhat of a puzzle to me because when he was at home with us, he seemed so sure of everything, but as soon as that front door opened, that sureness left him, and he became someone else.

"Pato, make sure that you watch over your brothers and sisters on the way to school today," Mama chimed as she always did before we left. Mama perceived me as ultimately responsible, and I was.

"Tina, have a good day at school," I said as I lovingly kissed her on the cheek, not having to wait one second for mine. Leaving Tina behind had always been hard for me ever since she had started going to the public school, which had a special program for the hearing and speech impaired. Tina was now better able to deal with herself and others because of the program.

"I'm almost ready for the bus," she mumbled, but her eyes told me that she wished that she could go with me and the others to our school, yet she couldn't, and wishful thinking wouldn't change a thing.

"I bet that I will beat you home from school," I said and laughed, wanting her to feel a part of the group even though we would be separated temporarily. Tina's mouth crinkled at the edges, breaking into a wide grin.

"How I love to see her smile," I mused to myself, turning abruptly around, now ready for whatever the morning might bring.

"Niños, your lunches," Mama reminded us as five outstretched hands hurriedly grasped a small paper sack that contained a taco or tortilla lovingly made by Mama. "It should be enough to last you until you get home," said Mama and smiled, knowing that she had to stretch every morsel we had, hoping that there would be enough. There usually was, but not always. "Samuel, don't forget your bat that you need for practice. It's half-hidden under yesterday's newspaper." Mama remembered everything.

Racing down the block, the five of us scurried along, tugging and darting in and out among one another, enjoying the brightness of the morning and kidding one another the way that brothers and sisters often do. After about two blocks, Samuel spied a group of kids huddled together as if in a football scrimmage.

"Pato, what do you think is going on up ahead?" he turned his head and nervously asked me, not really listening for my answer. Samuel didn't like it when bunches of kids were together because it usually signaled trouble. He certainly read it right today. From out of nowhere, a shriek of irritating taunting began.

"Well, look who's here––the Saenz clan who doesn't have a penny to their name. Just look at their clothes. It looks as though they have worn them for centuries." A jeering laugh began. Suddenly bits of rocks and debris were thick in the air. The girls began to whimper. Samuel stood as though he were in a time warp. He was frozen, completely unable to move. Tears of frustration and fear flooded his face.

"Samuel, take the girls, get out of here as fast as you can, and don't look back," I yelled, knowing that only I could stand my ground no matter how many kids there might be.

A big piece of dripping mud landed on my neck. I lost it, as Mama would say. I stopped completely and veered around.

"Show yourself if you are big enough to do it," I yelled furiously. As if right on cue, a rough-looking bunch of boys were on top of me, blocking my way, laughing at a silent joke that only they had heard.

"Pato, what's the matter with your brother and sisters?" Jose snarled. "Don't they want to stick around for the rest of the fun?"

That did it. Anyone could say anything about me, but when it came to my family, that was definitely off limits. I saw nothing but a big, overgrown bully whose time had come to be put in his place. I was the one to do it.

Jose, who was twice my size, suddenly grabbed the cotton collar cuff on the back of my shirt, spun me around, punched me in the back, and tripped me. I landed face down on clumps of Black-eyed Susan weeds that looked at me with their yellow and brown eyes, whispering that they were rooting for me. What happened next, I'm not sure, but I started punching wildly. My punches connected as the roar of chanting from Jose's bully friends began.

"Get him, Jose, get him good; wipe the road with him." The sounds burned my ears. Their words somehow allowed me to take control of the situation. On the ground, within my reach, I spied Samuel's bat, which he had dropped in his hasty retreat. I clutched it blindly, swinging without a care. The chanting stopped abruptly, and two of the boys, one on either side of me, tried to take the bat away. I was determined not to give it up. The bat was my only advantage.

Pedro, Jose's sidekick, yelled, "He's crazy, he's crazy; he's going to kill somebody." I suppose I would have if Jose had continued punching me. When Pedro called out, Jose became very aware of my uncontrolled rage and stopped.

Out of the bat's reach, Jose muttered, "Leave him alone for now," cocking his head in a bird-like fashion. His beady eyes flashed as he gasped, "This is just a taste of what is coming to you, little Pato." They were gone in a wink. I had to blink to make sure that they were really gone. Picking myself up out of the dirt, I assessed how much damage had been done, brushed myself off as best as I could, and trudged on to school. This episode was definitely not something that Mama needed to hear about. Making an aching promise to myself, I vowed to take care of Jose and the bullies alone, in my own way.

As I neared the school, it was an unforgettable moving sight: Aylvia, Amberina, and Avera had clasped hands and refused to go into the building until I showed my face in whatever condition it was in.

"I'm okay, girls; they hardly made a mark," I said as I tried to be very confident and comforting. After all, they were only girls reacting the way girls did around a fight––emotionally.

"Oh, Pato, you made it out alive. You were so brave. How we love you," cried Aylvia. That was all that I needed to hear. It was as if the girls had wrapped me in a huge bandage of love, healing me instantly inside and out.

"Samuel went on to his school after he made sure that we were safe," heaved Amberina as she trembled, awash with uncertainty, tossing her head around as her braids, bouncing back and forth, made a rhythm of their own.

"Pato, you are alive," shrieked Avera, the littlest of the girls, hugging me like she would never let go.

"Listen closely, girls. You're okay, and I'm okay, but now you need to get this totally out of your minds. Not a word to Mama, you hear?" I said as I gave them all a bear-like hug that only a brother could give. I smoothed their hair, adjusted their rumpled ribbons, and wiped off traces of tear stains on their shaken faces. A bit more soothed, my sisters sensed the urgency behind my words, glanced back, being assured that I was in one piece, then dashed off to their individual classes.

Remembering that fateful day was almost too much for me as I looked down at my white-clenched fists ready to pound anyone or anything that happened to get in their way; but thank goodness I was in my office with the door securely locked. It was a safe-haven, or so I tried to convince myself. Annoyed and fully aware that this was a completely different Jose, I finished checking my rosters. A slight cringe rippled through me as I realized how long I had been away from my classes due to my hospitalization. Getting back in front of my class after being out since November because of my open-heart surgery would be difficult, to say the least. It was now August of the new year. A lifetime had passed. A part of me wanted to come back, but another part dreaded it. The meetings, the other professors, the looks, the innuendos—I just didn't know whether I was up to the sparring like before. I was no longer invincible, and everyone knew it. Oh, to be back in sixth grade with Ms. Gulley when I could depend on others during the troubling times. As I slowly sipped my coffee, I could hear the whispers in the hallway on that fateful day at school after I had fought with José.

S.S. Simpson

The remainder of the morning went the way of a Monday morning; however, I sure did get several sneaky stares from some of the older boys who by now had heard every single detail of the fight, which had been categorized and glamorized, moment by moment, by Jose and his cronies.

"Pato, it's all around the school that Jose and his friends attacked you on the way to school today," whispered Carmen, looking down at the floor, shuffling her feet back and forth nervously on a squeaky floorboard. "How did you manage to hold them off and survive without anyone's help?"

While she spoke, Carmen tenderly placed one of her delicate soft, rose-colored hands on my shoulder, and I turned to melted mush.

Abruptly I declared inwardly that everything that occurred that morning had been worth it; I would have fought one hundred bullies to have Carmen's beautiful fingers wrapped around my shoulder.

"It was nothing," I replied, bursting with pride, trying not to reveal any tinges of pain from the pounding blows that had earlier rendered me nearly helpless. After our conversation the pain became bearable, and then I knew that I would make it. I did, until at lunch a menacing voice directly behind me said, "Pato, it isn't over; that was just a taste of what is coming to you." The voice was a dead giveaway. In my sleep, or rather my nightmares, I would recognize it. Just keep walking, I told myself, and I headed to Mr. Smith's natural science class, my last class of the day, the one that I knew would get my mind off today's events.

"Afternoon, Polo," Mr. Smith greeted me with one of his quizzical looks. "Glad to see that you are holding up so well."

"Sir, doing fine," I replied. Could he possibly know about the fight? Did teachers have an invisible communication line that enabled them to know what happened even on the way to school? I definitely needed to change our route.

"Class, get your materials ready because we are going out to the real classroom today, the great outdoors," stated Mr. Smith, who knew how much we all enjoyed exploring science that we could see, touch, and smell.

While we were outside looking for different kinds of leaves, since the lesson was based on leaf structure and function, Marie, one of my impulsive classmates, came barreling up to me with her hands stuffed with notes written on pink, yellow, and white paper sealed with big pieces of tape, which prevented prying eyes.

"What are these?" I asked, a bit dumbfounded as Marie breathlessly started to tell me how she had received them.

"All day long girls have been asking me to give these to you," she said as she shyly looked at me through her horn-rimmed glasses. "They all seem so worried about you, and I guess everyone knows that you and I have science together last period." She hesitated, as though she needed some reassurance, so I gave her a big smile.

"Thanks, Marie," I answered, realizing that it was an awkward thing for her to do because she had a major crush on me. How unbelievable when many of the scrawled names belonged to many female members of Jose's fan club. Jose's plan had completely backfired, because now I was getting all the gushing attention instead of Jose and his bullies. Before I knew it, the clanging ring of the last bell signaled the day's end. I stuffed the well-meaning notes in my pants, heading for Ms. Gulley's room. There Alyvia and I would tackle our after-school chores: emptying trash, sweeping floors, and doing any other odd jobs that arose. When my sisters and I were first granted admittance to Taylor Institute, one of the requirements was that we would have to work after school to offset our tuition. Bounding down the hallway, squished in the center of a group of girls, was Aylvia, who was a girl magnet pulling the others along. Spotting me, she couldn't reach me fast enough.

"Pato, you made it; I couldn't wait to see you," she burst Aylvia, looking at me as if I were her unbeatable hero for life, so I became one.

"Aylvia, hustle; we have to get our chores done. Did you forget?" I asked.

"Oh, the chores will always be there, but I needed to find out who is going out with Javier," she stubbornly replied.

As we neared Ms. Gulley's room, faint, whispering adult voices could be overheard that seemed to fade out just before we reached the door.

"Our students need to feel safe on their way to school," quipped one alto voice. "However, it is almost impossible to guarantee their safety if no adult is around," the voice continued. "Just because our school is located in a low-economic district doesn't mean the kids have to be scared. Safety first, no matter what; this is how I feel about it." The concerned voice suddenly stopped. For the second time that day, I felt my chest swell inside me like a helium balloon ready for takeoff. This voice undoubtedly belonged to one of our teachers. Just knowing that he cared that much about us was unnerving. Feeling funny and maybe a bit guilty for eavesdropping on the conversation, I coughed loudly and called out, "Ms. Gulley, I know that we are a little late, but where would you like us to start?"

There, leaning on her desk was her conversationalist, Mr. Spears, our beloved music teacher who always voiced his opinions on everything and believed that students were actually people, not programmed computers who made no mistakes. Mr. Spears quickly excused himself, although he took the time to rustle my hair as he passed by, telling Aylvia just how lucky she was to have a brother like me. Teachers have an uncanny habit of saying kind things when you least expect it, and this was one of those times.

"Polo and Aylvia, would you like some hard candy?" asked Ms. Gulley, handing me an oval jar full of assorted sweets: red fireballs that made your mouth smolder in a good way, green and yellow gumdrops that stuck together, horrifying other people. For an instant I guess Ms. Gully reminded me of Mama, knowing what I needed without my telling her; they were both mind readers, I decided. After jamming our mouths full, I spied a broom that had almost toppled out of her closet, which was crammed full of teacher cleaning stuff: a can of Old English cleaning fluid, assorted cloth rags with varying degrees of softness, buckets with handles, and boxes stuffed full of odds and ends. If I didn't know Ms. Gulley was a teacher, I would have thought that she was the custodian, recalling what she once told me, "Polo, it is better to be safe than sorry, to be prepared." She was probably prepared even for a hurricane, which could have occurred anytime during that time of year in the Rio Grande Valley.

"Aylvia, let's sweep the rooms first, then you pick up the trash in the even-numbered rooms, and I will collect the trash from the odd-numbered rooms." It was comfortable for me to take charge of a situation. Mama expected me to take on responsibility without being told how or what to do, so I did.

"Pato, let me just finish a few more of these chocolates," piped Aylvia, grabbing the broom, unwrapping the foiled kisses as though she had never eaten chocolate in her life. Mama once told me that girls crave chocolate at times, and this must have been one of those times. Before we knew it, we had said our goodbyes to Ms. Gulley, who never left school before five-thirty in the afternoon; maybe sometimes she didn't even leave. Could she have a folding cot in that closet as well?

Rounding the corner of our comfortable street, we anxiously clamored up the creaky front steps when we heard Samuel talking nervously to Mama. Holding our breath, we entered the uncertainty of the kitchen, giving Samuel a long, cold, questioning stare.

"Samuel, up for some ball before supper?" I asked, knowing I had to find out if he had revealed anything about the altercation to Mama.

"Sure, Pato, but I'm not sure where I left the bat," replied Samuel, giving me the chance to fill in the blanks, which I did.

"You forget everything," I quickly retorted without batting an eyelash. "Don't you remember on the way to school I asked you if I could borrow the bat because I wanted to play baseball with some of the other kids at school today?" With that blank look still on his face, Samuel's mouth opened and quickly closed, gazing at me in amazement.

To survive in the barrio, I had learned to think fast, making sure that whatever I said made sense.

"Boys, don't be too long out there in this heat," Mama reminded us.

"Samuel, what was all the chit-chat about with Mama?"

I rolled my eyes curiously, waiting for an answer, but with an older brother you couldn't seem too eager for any answer. Samuel grabbed me, throwing me down on the grass in a loving way, and said, "I really didn't know if I would see you again in one piece, with all of your parts connected in the right way." He breathed deeply. "I was sure that Jose probably had killed you. Pato, I was so scared. Sorry I wasn't much help this morning. I just couldn't think. It all happened so fast."

"Don't worry, Samuel. It's over. Hopefully it won't happen again anytime soon," I piped back. "Now, what about Mama?" I asked as we lay on our backs, gazing at the old mesquite tree whose branches overhung an eave on the back corner of the house. It was heavily laden with mesquite beans, which Mama used to make the sweetest jam that I ever tasted. I was hungry for food and answers from Samuel.

"Oh, the talk with Mama was about my stuff, things that are going on with me at school, specifically the fact that I don't much care for school. I'm thinking of dropping out and doing something else for a while," answered Samuel absentmindedly.

"What is so difficult about school?" I demanded, not believing what I had just heard. "All you have to do is listen in class and do whatever little homework that they assign you, but you need to do it and not worry so much about it," I said, trying to give Samuel a bolster of brotherly encouragement. All of a sudden, the fight lost its importance. All I cared about was helping Samuel stay in school.

"Don't worry, I'll figure something out. Have you talked to any of your teachers about what is troubling you? Maybe they could help make things smoother for you?" I suggested, trying to pick up his spirits.

"Pato, it just doesn't come that easily for me; the pressure during the day with the teachers and the kids, sometimes it's just too much for me." Samuel choked back some humiliation coated with angry tears. "Things are different for you; you don't care what people think because you put everything together the first time without so much as one minute of struggle. I've watched you, and that is how you work. I'm different. I spend a lot of time on things, and often my nerves just can't take it," Samuel said with a sad, faraway look on his face. Already knowing this about him, I guess I had hoped he would learn how to cope. He hadn't.

"Oh, Samuel, about the fight; let's just keep it between ourselves, agreed?" I asked, now feeling very guilty about being so concerned about myself, forgetting that each one of us had our own individual problems. Right now Samuel's was far more pressing than mine. "Here, throw me a few balls and let's see if I'm getting any better," I shouted to Samuel, hoping that if I got his mind off things for a while, he might be able to see things differently. "Great pitch. How do you curve those balls so easily? You are awesome at the mound." All he needed was just a little encouragement. During our short game, I couldn't concentrate at all, being more than ready when Mama called us in for supper.

"Pato, you're home," Avera and Amberina screeched in unison as they tumbled out the back porch doorway in their haste to get to me. Not knowing that I had gotten home from school, they had been waiting on the front steps, refusing to budge until Papa had informed them that Samuel and I were in the back.

"You made it through the day," Amberina said and sighed, usually expecting the worst before it had a chance to happen. Avera grabbed onto my pant leg and hung on as though for dear life. It was awkward getting all of that sisterly attention. While peering out of the kitchen window, Mama couldn't quite figure it out. Supper was quiet; I guess Papa thought that it was too quiet.

"Son, you can't seem to get comfortable in that chair. Anything hurting? Your back looks pretty stiff from here," Papa questioned as words flew out of my mouth.

"Got roughed up at the baseball game at school, Papa, that's all." I hoped that would be all, and it was. During our nightly Bible reading, Tina sensed that I was troubled and rested her head on my worn-out shoulder, causing my spirit to soar. There was no need for words.

THE ATTACKS

The stark walls where his numerous diplomas of achievement hung stared at me blindly. I still wasn't comfortable talking to a complete professional stranger about my private feelings.

"Doctor Saenz, you seem a bit withdrawn today, certainly not like your last visit when you were quite agitated and responded aggressively." I heard these clinical words tumbling out of Dr. Franco's mouth. Did he ever let the gates of his guard swing naturally without being swallowed in professional phrases? Evidently not.

"The panic attacks are becoming more frequent," I slowly replied, wondering how in the world anyone could understand what happened during one of these attacks: the terrifying, suffocating sensation. No amount of explaining would describe it, so I stopped trying.

"So, these attacks are causing you a great deal of concern?" commented the observing doctor.

"How in the world do you expect me to teach my class if I experience one of these attacks while I am lecturing?" I retorted. "It can't be done; there is too much at stake."

"That's an interesting statement. What do you mean by that?" Doctor Franco replied.

"I have a responsibility to my class to be fully prepared, consistent in my correctness, and flawless with my content," I answered. "How could you know what it is like when you have never been anyone's little soldier?" I said angrily to the doctor.

"That's an interesting phrase, but can you tell me what you mean by that?" Doctor Franco asked.

"It was Mama's pet name for me, which meant responsibility, one that never ended, like my Saturdays. On Saturdays I was appointed to do errands for Mama: going to the post office to drop off letters, paying the water and electric bills, and visiting the bank to check on her account. Of course, all of this was done on my makeshift bike, the one Papa had assembled from odds and ends of discarded bikes that he had found in the junkyard because we couldn't afford to buy a real one from the store. It only took him a week to put my bike together. When I first got it, I thought it was the greatest gift but then quickly started to hate it once I realized it was my errand mobile. Doing errands took up most of my time. Mama wanted to make sure that I had plenty to do, keeping my mind occupied and responsible. But there was this one Saturday ... I can still hear her."

"Pato, these bills can't walk into town; they need your help, and so do I," Mama said, encouraging me to begin my Saturday bicycle delivery express service. "First, I want you to make sure that you take this payment to the CPL office over on Lightway Road, which is the third right after you pass the intersection of Cable and Wirein," Mama instructed me. "After that, don't forget to stop at the bank, McAllen State Bank—you know, the one with the dome-shaped entrance—to deposit this money in my account." She encouraged me to talk to people I didn't know so that I would be able to handle myself in any situation, especially ones that involved money.

Without hesitation I replied, "Mama, don't worry, I will make sure that the payments are delivered carefully. You know that you can always count on me to get the task done." As I listened to what I had just said, it was like a recording on a well-worn tape that played and played and played. I was the one Mama relied on, the only one. The tape continued.

"Mijo, don't forget to be extra nice to Mrs. Hanes, the well-dressed, silver-haired lady at the bank; make sure that you give her a compliment or two, and look as though you mean it," Mama commented, giving me one of her looks as I jumped on my bike before she could add to the list. I thought about those people at the bank while peddling down the dirt roads speckled with tar. Maybe they had big, fancy parties every day because they were always dressed up with matching makeup and fingernail polish, and each strand of hair was molded, stuck in the right place. They were always expecting guests. As I breathed in the Saturday morning October air, my thoughts wandered back to Samuel and Jose, yet neither one did I want to think about. Now I just wanted to watch the gray and white mockingbirds dart back and forth as if in a crazy courtship dance that only they understood, listen to the mournful cry of the mourning dove trying to locate her mate, peer at the prairie dogs that scuttled in and out of the parched grasses along the road, and gaze at the crepe myrtle bushes adorned with soft hues of pink, white, and purple colors that hid bird nests with chirping occupants. When I was on my bike, I felt so carefree. My worries dropped off me like raindrops on willow branches after a soft mid-morning rain, the kind that you can smell as it washes newness into everything if you close your eyes just right. Before I knew it, the CPL building loomed ahead of me. Taking out the payment that was carefully tucked into my shirt pocket, I carefully deposited the envelope into the winding chute that swished the money away before I could change my mind. The whole process was so impersonal. It would be nice if the machine smiled or grinned or something, but it didn't; it just waited for me to finish, staring blankly at me as though it didn't care if it got the money or not. Boy, wouldn't it be nice not to have to worry about money, I thought to myself, yet I knew that worry would always be there.

"Your mama expected quite a bit from you, more than the others," interrupted Doctor Franco. "Would it be correct to say that you were the one who everyone leaned on, expecting you to come through regardless?"

"Haven't you been listening? I'm the only one who ever got anything done correctly on the first try, and no one stopped me, not even Jose," I said as I jerked around in my chair, feeling my hands sweat. "He tried to destroy me, but the more he tried, the harder I fought back, then I won, beat him back and broke him. He got a taste of his own bully medicine."

"You are saying that you and Jose had a final showdown, so to speak?" asked the doctor softly. He had dropped his guard. He really wanted to find out what happened to belittled Jose.

"It happened on that same Saturday after I went to the bank." I took a deep breath, continuing with my story.

"One down, one to go," I whispered out loud, thinking maybe I would get the errands done sooner today than most Saturdays, leaving time to re-wire the chicken coop that needed to be repaired. My chickens needed to feel safe in their coop at night-time. With my thoughts on the chickens, I forgot to speed up and get on the opposite side of the street as I neared Jose's house. Too late. I had been spotted. Jose and his cronies surrounded me. At the same time, a gray-speckled mockingbird shrieked and dove into a bush near me. That was not a good sign.

"Well, if it isn't scrawny Pato, all alone," said Septo, Jose's hammer-man, not someone you wanted to tangle with. His hands looked like overgrown hammers, so the name fit.

"Hammer, get out of my way. I don't have time to bother with you today; I am on a tight schedule; people to see, things to do," I heard myself say as Hammer just stood there laughing at me like I was joking. But I wasn't. "Hammer, I have just been to the bank, and now I have another important appointment that I need to keep, so if you will please excuse me, I will be on my way," I continued because I had no idea what I was going to do.

"I don't see any bats around this time, so I guess you will just have to show us what you are really made of," replied Hammer, dragging me off my bike and shoving me toward Jose's yard where at least six other gloating boys stood just waiting for the inevitable showdown.

"Well, if it isn't the bat-swinging wild man on this sunny Saturday morning. This will be your last Saturday morning, so enjoy it while you can," muttered Jose. I realized I was very much alone and very batless. Suddenly a voice deep within me shouted that I might be able to do this.

Hammer, who led the rest of the boys, had encircled Jose and me. My luck, however, changed drastically.

"Marco, get the gloves. They are in the garage. I can't wait to make mincemeat out of brave little shrimpy Pato," said Jose, who was whistling an irritating tune from one of the mob movies, which I'm sure he belonged in. When I heard the word gloves, it was the most wonderful word that I could have heard. My heart started pounding, my adrenalin raced, and my mind became completely focused. Unbeknown to Jose and the rest of his boys, I was an ace at boxing. Samuel and I sparred whenever we got a chance, and I usually was the one who remained standing, even though Samuel was much bigger and stronger than I was.

"Boy, I can't wait to see you pound Pato into the ground, Jose," Pedro shouted, taunting me right in my face. "How long do you think it will take? One minute, two, three at the most?" When Pedro stuffed my hands into the gloves and roughly laced them up, a certain calmness overtook me. I wasn't afraid. All that I could hear was Samuel's voice: "Watch his hands, back him into a corner, keep your hands up, and most important look into his eyes and show no fear." That's just what I did. All I could see were two squinting, piercing eyes that bulged in and out and two long grappling arms wrapped tightly at the wrist with tape, looking for their target.

"Get him, Jose, wipe him out, take him down," the other degenerates shouted in deafening unison. After the first "get him," I didn't hear a word. Jose swung hard up to the right, missed my jaw by about an inch, stumbled backward, almost losing his balance, and then swung wildly at my chest. Every determined punch missed me. I was very scrawny, but I could move, and move I did. Then it came, the golden opportunity of any boxing match, when you had your opponent. Jose couldn't connect any of his punches and was getting very frustrated because of my jumping around, a bit like Joe Lewis. Jose dropped his hands for a moment; leaving himself wide open. Putting as much oomph as I possibly could into my right glove, which was now positioned directly in front of Jose's nose, like a mark on a hunting target, I shot my right hand into his face. Blood went everywhere, gushing out of Jose's face. Jose hit the ground in a thud without moving a muscle. All around me were terrified screams.

"You killed him, you killed him!"

Maybe I did, but somehow I figured Jose got what he deserved. After all, he came after me, so I felt entirely justified for a split second––but only for a second. Looking down, I realized that he truly was motionless. However, within a minute Jose started wailing worse than Samuel, if that were possible.

"You broke my face; I can't breathe; what have you done to me?" Jose managed to gurgle out as he choked and sobbed uncontrollably. I stared at him as the bully shriveled away. In his place was a frightened, overgrown, helpless twelve-year old who needed my help, imagine, my help. As if I hadn't been pulled apart enough for one hour, I thought, but I guess I hadn't. My thoughts raced ahead of me, waiting for me to catch up with them, and I did.

"Get me some rags and water quickly; there is no time to waste," I commanded the rest of the speechless, scared, shrinking bullies. Quickly scanning the area, I spied a faucet above some old boards near Jose's house. "Bring him over here."

Septo fastened his shaking arms around Jose's lifeless legs, while Pedro cupped his arms under his left side and Marco positioned himself under his right side.

"When I count to three, pick him up ... one, two, three." The deed was done. With Jose's face tilted back and my fingers holding his nose, I somehow managed to stop the furious bleeding after applying pressure with some blood-soaked rags that I found stuffed in a corner in Jose's garage. It seemed as if they knew that I needed them. As Jose's sobbing calmed down, he looked at me with petrified eyes.

"Am I going to die?"

"No, but maybe you should," I said, and then Jose started bawling again, so I whispered, "Hey, I was only kidding; you will be fine, but you might need a new nose."

It was then that I saw it: the total surrender in Jose's eyes, not the big-shot, overconfident, obnoxious, jeering bully. Humility looked up at me. Jose knew he had been beaten, beaten well. An awakening rose from deep within me. Bullies are not to be feared but confronted, regardless of their shape or size. But the awakening told me that Mama could not find out about this, not ever.

"That ability to confront, that control, it has all slipped away. The inner strength, the desire has disappeared, as if it never existed," I said as I got up.

Doctor Franco's time was up, and I didn't need to hear him obnoxiously confirm it.

No Chimneys in the Barrio

Nestled comfortably in a cushioned chair that was tucked under a swaying palm tree on our back porch, I could hear the harmonious clanging of the metal wind chimes playing a tuned chorus when the wind blew. Sara was cuddling with one of her six splotched kittens that we had unintentionally inherited when a hungry neighbor's pregnant mother cat was given to us. Sara fed her. She became Sara's. One stormy evening at three o'clock in the morning the very pregnant mother cat gave birth to three sets of identical twins. The chosen location was a six-inch deep garden hole directly beneath our bedroom window. Quickly filling with water, the hole was anything but a safe haven. A heart-stopping mewing filled the night air. Within seconds Sara bounded out into the windy downpour, snatched the newly born twins, and relocated them to a warm throw rug in the garage. Terrified, the mother cat watched in horror yet instinctively knew that Sara was trying to help and quickly followed her drenched newborns. From that day forward, the love affair grew tenderly between the mother cat, her kittens, and their guardian Polo. As I watched Sara tenderly talking to her kittens as though they understood her, I suddenly felt my chest heave and was unable to breathe. Gasping for air, I fell off the cushion. Startled, Sara lunged for me and caught me in her arms. After being heavily escorted inside, I calmed down, realizing it must have been an asthma attack from the heavy pollen that laced the air. But Sara's rebound took longer.

"You never told me that you had asthma. How come you never mentioned that you had trouble breathing?" she prodded, going on and on. She did that when she felt strongly about something. I wasn't a sharer of information, especially sickness. As I searched her anxious face, I knew that she deserved to have the blanks filled in, so I told her about Doctor Cossos.

"Pato, just try to relax and don't fight it," whispered Doctor Cossos, who had a steady, soothing voice that echoed in my ears as the panic arose in me time and time again. I was fighting for air, unable to breath, fairly certain that I was going to die.

"I can't breathe," I cried as my body shook and my lungs ached. Mama tried to comfort me while Doctor Cossos looked for an entry spot on my buttocks with the dreaded needle. My arms were too skinny for poking.

"Pato, my dear Pato," Mama said softly, "it will be over before you know it, I promise you," Mama whispered, tenderly wiping my forehead with a wet cloth and removing my soaked shirt. "It is an asthma attack, Pato, nothing else," said Mama, silently stroking my arms, knowing just how terrifying one could be since she suffered from them as well as a child.

"All right, Pato, here we go," piped the good doctor as he filled the needle full of epinephrine and directed it toward my quivering left buttock. Suddenly it was done; the shot pierced my skin, and the clear fluid rushed inside, looking for closed bronchial tubes, opening them up. I could feel the sweet sensation of air rush easily into my lungs. I gulped and gulped again.

"I can breathe," I managed to get out while Mama turned to Doctor Cossos and said, "Vaya con Dios, Doctor Cossos. You have saved my son, and I will always be grateful to you for coming to our house, even though it is very late and the weather is very bad."

"That was the beginning of my asthma attacks. Using Mama's method of treatment––inhaling steam from boiling water on the stove and inhaling Vicks Vapor Rub that had been smeared all over my chest and underneath my nose, I learned to control them."

"Is that why you hate the smell of Vick's Vapor Rub when I use it?" asked Sara, now knowing why I never wanted to get near her when she had rubbed the smelly, clear vapor under her own nose when she was sick.

"Yes, I can't stand the odor. It makes me remember."

Sara's eyes were now shining brightly because I had taken the time to share, which I didn't usually do.

"Now that you are breathing better, there is something else that has always puzzled me. Whenever I ask you what you would like for your birthday or Christmas, you usually say 'Nothing,' and you mean it. You never get excited about gifts, what they are, or who they are from. How come?" Sara loved gifts and would stare at them for hours, never in any hurry to open them.

"Gifts are not something that I am comfortable with. As a boy I wanted and needed things but usually didn't get them. We were so poor that there was no money for extras. There was this one Christmas when I realized that it didn't matter."

In a few days it would be Christmas. After listening to my brother's and sisters' want lists for Santa, I knew Santa would be very busy. We were poor, but at Christmastime we thought dreams might come true if Santa listened closely enough. That is when I decided to help Santa out since Santa didn't slide down chimneys in the barrio. There weren't any.

Saving every penny and bargaining my life away, I was able to complete most of the lists and get most of the gifts. On Mama's and Papa's list there was only one wish: for each one of us to get educated so that we could live in a neighborhood that had chimneys.

But on that Christmas Eve I became aware of my own gift, the power to attract women. On this night, Samuel, Aylvia, and I, who were the oldest, had a chance to meet and mingle with other kids from the Valley's Methodist Youth Group. Our mission was to delight members of the

Methodist Church with traditional Christmas carols. Before we had any more time to warm up our voices, we were at the church, and older kids, mostly Samuel's age, were piling out of cars. Girls were popping their heads in the rearview mirrors for one last makeup check as boys stuffed the scarves their mother's made them wear in the inside of their jackets. Mints were a must as couples emerged. Aylvia and I, being a few years younger, stared in amazement, wondering if that was our future. Yet we followed suit and checked our breaths as well.

"Samuel, aren't you going to introduce me?" said a soft, sweet, slippery voice from out of nowhere.

"Sure, Libby, this is my little brother, Pato, uh, Pato this is Libby." Fate had introduced me to a beautiful girl with long, wavy, brownish-blond tinted hair that hid a clear-skinned, high-cheek-boned face. Her confident, coffee-colored eyes fastened onto me like a button on a shirt. What came out of my mouth had to be wonderful, and it was:

"Are you cold? Would you like to borrow my scarf?" I asked as the wind cooperated, gusting mightily. Libby couldn't refuse and didn't.

"Pato, how sweet of you. You're so cute. Samuel never told me he had such an adorable younger brother," Libby slowly said while I hung onto her every word like an upside-down bat. No one had ever spoken to me in that manner or tone before, but I quickly snapped out of it.

"Polo is really the name that I go by, yet Samuel sometimes calls me Pato," I replied, looking confidently into Libby's eyes, hoping that I sounded very mature. I guess I did. She grabbed my hand and never let go. I was sure that I was in heaven.

Aylvia quickly evaporated after spying some of her friends. She couldn't quite understand why this girl was making such a fuss over me. She would have to take a closer look at me tomorrow. Maybe something had changed.

While we were caroling, Libby was very much at ease, making me feel as if I were twenty. Being a very thin kid and small for my age, I never thought of myself as particularly good looking, certainly not someone an older woman would want to be with ... except Mama. But if Mama could see me now, she would kill me. During our last carol, we were invited into Mr. Martin's home where there were things that I had never seen before: walls lined with fancy wallpaper and no peeling paint, soft, velvety sofas with billowing pillows, gold-leaf mirrors, portraits of children lining the stairwell, and a huge mahogany table that overflowed with cups of hot chocolate loaded with whipped cream, cylinder-shaped sugar doughnuts, chocolate brownies loaded with walnuts, and Christmas napkins that had Santas on them.

"Help yourselves, young people," Mr. Martin motioned to us. "Let me get the Mrs. so that she can hear how wonderful you sound." After we sang some favorites of the Martins, we caroled our way back to the parking lot. Parents were eagerly waiting for us and acted like we had been gone for weeks, visiting faraway places where only teenagers were allowed.

Departing, I had to let go of Libby's hand but vowed not to wash mine until I saw her again.

"Pato, hey, is it all right if I call you that now?" asked Samuel, who was at the wheel of Papa's fifty Ford, feeling very grown up himself. "Libby really liked you immediately. I've never seen her act quite like that before." Samuel hesitated, still not quite believing what he had just witnessed.

"Yeah, she was pretty cool," I replied nonchalantly.

"Well, Samuel, what do you expect," piped Aylvia. "It is in the genes; not the blue jeans but the other kind, the ones that you are born with." She decided to examine me tonight instead of tomorrow.

That night when I looked in that old broken mirror, I saw something I had never seen before: a budding glow, a confidence that I had heard someone call charisma. That glow was still there in the morning when I heard shrieks of joy and merriment as the wanted gifts were found.

"Oh, what a beautiful dolly, and she looks a little like me," shouted Amberina, full of amazement. Avera, what did you get?" Amberina asked hastily, her eyes brimming with love for her sister, hoping that Avera also got a doll and not a pair of socks, underwear, or other items that she needed.

The excitement level reached a new pitch as Avera shredded the paper quickly and exclaimed, "I also got a doll, but one with long, blond hair like some of my Anglo friends at school. It was a term derived from the word Anglo-Saxon, which meant white. Here in the Valley it screamed of rank, denoting the absence of Mexican blood in one's lineage. My older sisters, Tina and Aylvia, were hoping for something other than dolls and were not disappointed. A few weeks earlier, Samuel and I pooled our money together because my bargaining power ran out. Tina and Aylvia both received matching music boxes with twirling ballerinas dressed in pink tutus and rose-colored ballet shoes. The best part of the music box was that only a secret key could open it. Girls love keys and secrets. It gives them a sense of power. In our family they needed it.

"Mama, Papa, look at the twirling figurines and listen. They play 'Silent Night,'" whispered Aylvia and Tina together. They were breathless and carefully holding the music boxes as though they might somehow interrupt the trumpeting and fluting sounds of the musical strands. Mama and Papa gave Samuel and me one of their looks, full of teary thankful wonder because there were just too many of us for them to surprise. They were grateful to have two extra Santas around.

But even Santas can be surprised, and we were.

"Papa, I love it; it is the most wonderful bike that I have ever seen, but how in the world did you find it?" Samuel cried in amazement as he hurriedly ripped off bits of paper that were taped to the bike, examining every inch of it. Matching streamers of red and blue puffy plastic jetted out of both ends of the awesome handlebars.

"Pato, check this out. Isn't it the neatest bike in the world?" declared Samuel, quite overwhelmed, gurgling like a just-turned-on fountain. Mama called me into the kitchen where she was busy preparing her bunuelos, a Christmas tradition made with flour tortillas that are fried then loaded with gobs of fattening butter and sprinkles of cinnamon. As I reached out for one, she put her arms around my waist and said, "Pato, we didn't have enough for two bikes, but with Samuel being the oldest and having so much trouble at school..." Her voice wobbled a little.

"Mama, I know. Besides, I already have a bike," I reassured her and meant it. "Maybe now Samuel can help out with the errands." I smiled, and that did it. Mama just grabbed me and cried.

"Pato, my little solider, how I love you so; you are really becoming quite mature lately," Mama said, sobbing softly.

"I know, Mama, I am developing charisma, but if only I could grow a bit faster," I told her.

"It will come," she whispered lovingly. "All in due time."

Sara gave me one of those looks of hers, full of questioning and empathy. She knew only too well the vast chasm that separated our childhoods. Hers was one of privilege, and mine was one of survival. My recounting of a Christmas past just reinforced her determination to make me feel privileged because I had her love.

CROCUSES

D eciding to take Dr. Franco's advice, I filled my prescription of
tranquilizers, which was supposed to ease my panic attacks, giving
me a sense of calmness and renewal. Thoughts of renewal brought to mind
stirrings of springtime when I was a boy.

You could tell that spring hung in the air, and that meant chasing. The
bees buzzed non-stop, searching for one another, the mockingbirds did
a dip and dive show, determined to win their audience, the prairie dogs
popped in and out of their burrows like they were being timed, but girls,
girls were the best at it.

"Pato, Mellin is coming over in a few minutes to join us in a game
of hide-and-seek," said Avera, pointing her finger in the direction of the
house across the street. "I told her you would be joining us in the game.
Will you?" she eagerly asked as though her entire friendship with Mellin
depended on my answer.

"Sure, let's round up everybody else. It will be more fun because the
more people that play, the harder it is to find places to hide," I responded.
"Samuel, Aylvia, Amberina, Tina, join in on a game of hide-and-seek. But
I am making the game more adventurous. Everyone has to carry one of
these little tingling bells that I found yesterday in a discarded box on the
vacant lot next to us."

Tito, the youngest, who heard the commotion, poked his little head out of the doorway, giggling and drooling on his handmade matching plaid shorts outfit. That only added to his cuteness, which I remembered was in the genes, but not the kind you wear. While the game was underway, Mellin became attached to my side and had no intention of leaving. That surprised me because she was only eight years old. After assuring her that I wouldn't vanish, she finally left as the rest of the players had already quit. The next day, as I carefully lifted up the black metal top of the mailbox, 1spied a letter addressed to me written on notebook paper that was carefully folded in two. It was placed on top of the other letters, so I opened it and absentmindedly started reading it. I was interested after reading the first line, but then I stared in disbelief.

"Dear Pato, please check the box below that tells how you feel about our relationship."

Relationship? I panicked. What relationship? Who was this from? I raced to the bottom of the letter and found the key. It was signed Mellin from across the street. Heaving a big sigh of relief, I stuffed the paper in my pocket and spotted Aylvia in the front yard playing with her music box.

"Hey, Aylvia, check this out," I cheerfully called to her as her ears pointed upward like a hunting dog ready to get a whiff of its prey, and that is exactly how I felt––like Mellin's prey.

"Pato, don't you know that young Mellin has a major crush on you," spouted Aylvia as she read the directions on the letter. "Check the box that tells how you feel," she read on. "Box 1: I like you a lot; Box 2: we should go steady; and Box 3: let's just be friends," finished Aylvia. "Pato, what do you do to these girls?" she said after giving me a sisterly grin.

"Aylvia, isn't this a bit unusual for an eight-year-old girl to do this?" I queried.

"No, Pato, not at all. I remember when I told Philipe that I would go steady with him after I had only spoken to him once, so he gave me a makeshift ring, and I wore it around my neck, but then I never talked to him again. Guess what? I still have the ring."

"Oh," I moaned, "but you have to fix it for me. Swear on yourself, Aylvia."

"I swear, but you are the one who wanted the charisma, and it looks like it is in full bloom." Right then and there, I made up my mind that I would learn how to control this hypnotic addiction that girls felt for me. But it was just the onset.

News of crushes must travel very fast. Since I declined advances from Libby, Aylvia's friends started popping up like crocuses at the front door.

"Pato, can you get the door for me, please? It's Valerie from next door," Aylvia, who was applying her makeup, shouted urgently. I wondered why girls had to cover up their faces. They must not like them, I thought. Aylvia quickly rushed out, and the gabbing began. It was as if they hadn't seen each other in a year, but they saw each other every day at school. Anxious for quietness, I quickly headed for our mulberry tree, which was loaded with sweet ripe mulberries that intoxicated the air with their lavender scent. Sitting under this tree was a favorite pastime of mine. It gave me needed privacy. Before I knew it, Valerie had positioned herself beside me as if it were a skilled maneuver.

"Pato, it's great to see you again," started Valerie. I wasn't really interested in what she was saying and plucked berries, eating them as fast as I could pull them off the tree. But Valerie was determined, making eye contact with me even though I tried to resist. It was useless. I couldn't control the monster; the charisma had leaked out again. I guess she was okay for an older girl, pretty much like my sister. She had a very natural way about her and made me laugh easily and effortlessly. But Valerie was Aylvia's friend. Where was Aylvia? Then I got it. She wanted to talk to me, and Aylvia was just an excuse. I was the reason. I shuddered at the realization, determined to be conveniently absent when knocking crocuses appeared at the door.

I chuckled out loud, knowing how women were drawn to me, much to Sara's dismay. Usually when we were out doing necessary errands like purchasing cat food, we ran into former students of mine. Invariably female, they would ooh and ah over me like I was a long-lost friend who needed to be found. It usually took ten minutes before their speech rate came within the speed limit. With Sara's glaring eyes, I knew that I had reached my limit.

I am secretly delighted that my former students take the time to acknowledge and relate their present achievements to me. Sara, on the other hand, can't understand it. Then I lovingly remind her it was my charisma that attracted her in the very same way. But I wasn't always charismatic. My thoughts drifted back to when I annoyed others with my irritating behavior.

I couldn't help it. Three-year-old Tito was getting cuter by the minute as he shook his golden, wavy locks of hair. Dressed in a freshly starched white, short-sleeve shirt with matching white shorts, Tito looked like he needed to be messed up. I had the job qualifications and knew he had to toughen up so he wouldn't grow up girly or worry about getting dirty.

"Tito, take a look at this puddle," I said and motioned to him. "Watch me jump over it," I said and cleared it by a mile. Tito watched intently, wanting to be just like me.

"Can't do it," he said, frowning, needing a little more encouragement.

"Sure you can," I repeated, doing it again. It worked. I had kindled his courage curiosity. He tried it. A big mistake. Poor Tito landed in the middle of the puddle, right in the muddiest part. Dripping with gooey mud and sudden fear, Tito wailed as though he had been shot. Shrieking with horror, Tito knew his brand new clothes were ruined. Because he cried so hard, I actually felt a little guilty, especially when Mama came barreling out of the house, terrified.

"Mama, Tito fell into the mud," I said sheepishly. Mama gave me a terrible look full of loathing as her eyes brimmed over with tears. Suddenly it wasn't so funny. I wanted to throw up.

"When your Papa gets home ..." She didn't need to say anymore. I knew what was coming. But being locked out of the house for the rest of the day didn't hurt me nearly as much as seeing Mama's face. That haunted me. I hated myself and what I had done. I vowed to let nature take its course and not try to make a man out of Tito before his time.

CHANGES

"I don't think that I want to return to the pressure spiral at school," blurted out Sara as she sipped her soothing ice tea, cuddling Creamy, her favorite of the kittens. He was a spunky, cream-colored male who had green, seaweed eyes that reminded her of the ocean when the sun shone on them. With school only a few weeks away and being a middle-school teacher, she was unraveling like a ball of yarn. For a brief moment, I considered offering her one of my calming tranquilizers then thought better of it. Sara abhorred medicine of any kind, refusing even to take an aspirin when she was in pain. With all of my medicine bottles, our kitchen counter looked like a pharmacy, which bothered her. She resented it. The pills were always in her way.

"Don't you remember last summer when you told me the same thing at about the same time? You weren't up to the six o'clock wake-up call and all that followed. Yet once you got back into the routine, you were fine?" I reminded her, hoping that she would make the needed connection. "Thinking back I will never forget my own dreaded passage: going from a well-respected sixth grader to a lowly, shunned-upon seventh grader in middle school. Now that took some readjusting."

Graduation was upon us, a time of uncertainty and tears, especially for the girls. Carmen, my affectionate friend, was seated beside me in one of the back rows of the chapel. As diplomas were passed out, Carmen nudged closer and closer to me like a scared bird seeking reassurance.

"Carmen, do you remember the Bible verse reading contest and how I was certain that I wouldn't be able to memorize a complete passage? Mama and Papa drilled me every night as I recited my way through the Psalms. Much to everyone's amazement, especially Ms. Gulley's, I won the contest after I recited perfectly not one passage but three. I was so scared, yet the words just tumbled out of my mouth because I had developed some much-needed confidence. Now it is so easy for me to memorize; in fact it is fun," I said, remembering when an engraved Bible with golden edges was placed in my unexpected hands. "Then the time when Mr. Smith took a group of us on the overnight camping trip to Benson Park, showing us how to pitch a tent, make a fire by rubbing twigs together, and appreciate nightly sounds? At first, Carmen, you were really scared, but then once you began to understand what creatures were making the sounds, you even enjoyed the creepy ones." I gazed at her tenderly as I had that night.

"Yes, you're right, but there was a time when I stayed scared because of what happened to you. It was back in third grade. Actually, we might have been sitting right here in this very pew. It was after the Wednesday chapel service when Reverend Brown asked anyone who wanted to seek the Lord and change his ways to come up to the front of the altar and kneel before him. I didn't know what to do."

"I will never forget it," I said once again, feeling my trembling knees on the velvet carpet in front of Reverend Brown and my Lord. "That day the Lord saved me from killing myself or someone else. My fighting, my anger, my pain, it was uncontrollable. In those ten minutes it all stopped. I was changed."

"You were sobbing, shaking, and deeply moved. You told me that you felt the Lord reach inside you," Carmen said gently, nudging my knee. "All I remember is that you couldn't stand up for a while. I thought you were going to be violently sick, so I rushed up and didn't dare leave your side until Reverend Brown helped you into the foyer where you recovered somewhat."

"So you see, there have been times when we were unsure what was going to happen. But we have always been there for each other, and we always will be. The school and grade doesn't matter. Just imagine the adventures that await us at middle school."

"Pato, you are convincing and hopefully right. Next year will be challenging, but as long as you are there ..."

"Whatever happened to Carmen, the girl you were so close to so long ago?" Sara asked me with a distant look in her eyes, recalling what a terrible transition it had been for her as well when she went to middle school. It was her undoing, and she loathed it.

"I'm afraid that crusty weeds have crept between old school friends and me. I have never had the time nor taken the time to do the essential weeding. I wish now that I had. Occasionally I will see a familiar face on television, a pharmacist or someone running for office, but I guess events in my life have put distance between who I used to be and who I am now." I sighed, realizing just how much I had changed even since my collegiate days at the University of Texas. "I have always tried hard to achieve, working even during the summers, which meant no free time for me or others. I can still remember that first back-aching summer that Mama taught us the value of work. It became a part of me."

If I thought summer vacation meant more free time, I was very wrong. Within the first days of freedom, Mama put us to work, hard backbreaking work. It turned out to be a family affair with Mama supervising. Papa was busy doing his own supervising as a head mechanic working full time at Best Motors. Mama made sure that we got up with the sun and didn't return until midday. Work meant the field, which belonged to friends of Mama and Papa. Hot, humid, scorching sun burned your head, face, neck, and anything else that wasn't covered. Each one of us dragged a makeshift burlap bag up and down rows of mature cotton that begged to be plucked correctly. I learned the hard way that if you did it too fast you would get stickers in your hands. If you were too slow, you would get harassed by everyone else who was trying to keep a certain pace. Getting behind meant harassment and extra picking. You had to have a certain amount of cotton in your sack if you wanted to get paid. Picking cotton was the hardest thing that I had ever done before in my life. I hated it. Mama would no longer want to lovingly stroke my hands. Examining them I began to see crevices like cracks in the sun-parched soil. It sickened me. My hands were made to hold a pen, pencil, or book––not sticky puffs of stubborn cotton. I devised a scheme to put an end to this daily morning ritual. Once Mama had trained us, we initiated the routine ourselves. Piling into Samuel's car, we headed for the waiting field that was five miles away.

The scheme began to take on a life of its own. It was the last morning that I was going to be a victim of summer, of poverty, and of circumstance. As I looked around, there were no blond-haired heads bobbing between the cotton plants nor white hands reaching for the white, fluffy commodity. There were only dark faces with dark hair that reached with dark hands. These were the fieldworkers, the only ones that had do this type of work, the Mexicans.

"Aylvia, you don't look good," I said as I bent over and squeezed my head between the cotton plants, getting a good glimpse of Aylvia, who was in the row next to me dragging her sack.

"I'm okay, Pato," she answered while wiping swirls of sweat from her forehead.

"No, you look sick. Isn't it that time for you, you know when you stomach hurts?"
I asked her.

"No," she said, but then she got it. "You're right. It is that time, and I think Tina is feeling sick also," she giggled and continued, "How did you know, Pato? I was hoping that you would be able to come up with something to get us out of this."

That day Mama was very surprised to see Samuel's car barreling up the dirt driveway only an hour after leaving. Watching the girls' drama, Mama agreed that we didn't have to return to finish our daily torture. After witnessing a few days of various illnesses, Mama decided that we had picked enough cotton and learned her objective.

"Now you understand what hard labor is like. I want each of you to know that if you don't finish school or have some type of job, this is what your future holds for you—sticky cotton." Her eyes bore into each of ours like a drill finding oil. Her point was never forgotten. To this day I hate being out in the sun.

———————————

"Did you have a chance to do anything fun that summer once your hands healed?" questioned Sara, feeling guilty since she never had to work a summer in her life. Her hands never had crevices.

"Well, there was Bible school that allowed me to experience things that I never knew existed. The Salvation Army offered this program to young people, mostly underprivileged kids like us, where you could learn arts and crafts, music, and of course scripture from the Bible. But this expedition didn't require Samuel's chauffeuring. It was just down the street. We walked. The building was very unassuming, gray-black, windowless, but inside was excitement, new ways of doing things, and kids who were worse off than we were. It allowed each of us a chance to examine ourselves and realize what we did have. A wonderful door was suddenly yanked wide open for us. It was musical and changed my life forever.

"Samuel, try this. It's a trombone that has a sliding stick that you move back and forth while you blow and press these three valves down with your other hand." I picked up the awkward instrument and handed it to him.

"Pato, do you really think they can teach me how to play it? It looks complicated," said Samuel, feeling suddenly challenged.

Aylvia was drawn to the clarinet and eagerly wanted the chance to work the numerous keys with her fingers. As I examined other instruments, a shiny bugle, properly called a cornet, caught my eye and coaxed me to tighten my lips around its mouthpiece. Simultaneously I pumped the valves, hearing the most beautiful notes imaginable. Never again would I be the same.

Putting the instruments aside, Tina, Avera, and Amberina opted for arts and crafts, making a beeline for the crafts table that was covered with woven pot holders, handmade lanyards, and other cleverly-made items.

Each one of us found individual doors that led to individual challenges, stirring our curiosity, making us better.

For me the musical door never closed. Ms. Miller, who just happened to hear me play at the Bible Institute, suggested that I take lessons with her at the Salvation Army, so my trumpet saga began. Mrs. Miller was an accomplished musician herself, and nothing gave her more pleasure than to tutor talented underprivileged kids who otherwise couldn't afford lessons. So with daily workouts my flexible fingers and puckered lips were ready when school started. Nothing could hold me back.

The band hall was crowded with numerous boys and girls each clutching their pride and joy, their cornet. Each one was determined to impress Mr. Able, the school's band director, so that he would choose them to warm up one of the sought-after chairs in the trumpet section. You could almost see them drooling with expectation. As I looked around, I couldn't help but notice that I was surrounded by the others, the Anglos. I wondered if you had to be white to try out, but no one asked me to leave, so I stayed. Jeering laughs and fingers were pointed at me behind my back, but I saw them, and it only fueled my determination. I was suddenly pulled out of my thoughts when I heard my name announced over the loudspeaker. Not knowing if it was good or bad to be first, I watched my feet carry me up the stairs toward the stage. Mr. Able didn't seem surprised when he saw me, so I decided then and there that I would show all the whites how a Mexican boy could play the cornet. As I played it grew very quiet as a soft hush rippled through the room. A big grin spread across his face, one of intoxication and delight. He couldn't get enough. After I finished he escorted me to the first chair and told me from then on it was up to me to keep it warm. Suddenly I didn't have to prove anything to anyone. I was given the opportunity to lead, and I did. Solos were mine. The lights dimmed, the spotlight glowed, and expectant faces waited but seemed startled that a minority was in the spotlight and not one of their own. But I owned the room, and not an eye left my face. Free-flowing magical rhythms transfixed the audience, allowing their spirits to soar. The gift was mine, and I gave it up freely. Music transcended the barrios. I was no longer labeled. Drowning in my music, I was equal.

The Worn Shoebox

"P olo," I heard a gasp from my wife, "what is this that I found upstairs next to your study under the sink?" She held out a much weathered, worn shoebox that I had made in seventh grade during my one and only try at shop class.

"That is one of the purest forms of self-expression, Sara. It is the only thing that I was able to make. I will never forget that class or my instructor, Mr. Nailin."

I can still hear the dull pounding of the hammers controlling the shop room. All I could smell was the pungent odor of freshly-hewn woodchips mingled with fumes of just-opened paint. It made me sick to my stomach. A wood-making shop class was definitely not where I belonged. The only reason that I had signed up for this class was to be with my newly-found friends, a small group of barrio boys who were just like me, or so I thought. In seventh grade friends were critical to your survival, especially since many of the other students were Anglos. As I craned my neck to get a glance at Roberto's bookcase, I actually saw an almost completed, respectable bookcase that any book would be proud to be on. On the other hand, or shoe, when I looked at my best attempt at a shoebox, I felt sorry for any shoe that had to depend on this box for its survival. Try as I might, this poor makeshift box still looked as though I had started it yesterday, even though I had been working on it for weeks. My friends offered their encouragement, but I knew that it was futile because my hands were just not made to hold a hammer or a paintbrush. My suspicions were confirmed when I received a D for my shop grade, but not before I was singled out by Mr. Nailin for one of his famous hall talks.

"Polo, I have watched you struggle for weeks trying to put together your project. I am very curious why you signed up for this class when it is quite evident that this is not your forte. Your hands were not meant for assembling pieces of materials to form a whole," said Mr. Nailin, who motioned me to hold out my hands, which I did. "Just look at your long, slender fingers. They need to be holding pens, books, and cornets, but not tools, never tools, Polo." I couldn't have agreed with him more. Once I got home and Papa saw my grade, I had another conversation, but it wasn't in a hall; it was in front of many other ears and eyes.

"How can you fail a shop class when it requires very little studying? All you have to do is put things together?" Papa was horrified but finally realized that I was not going to be just like him, an ace car mechanic who could get his hands dirty, understand everything under a car hood while tuning it up. He wanted so much for me to do manly things. I guess he was afraid that I would become too girly with my books and spotless fingernails. Although when I showed Papa my shoebox, he just kept turning it this way and that, not saying a word. I knew that he was shocked, wounded, and disappointed. But I was wrong. Years later I found my shoebox neatly tucked under his bed. Opening it, I found polishes, rags, and various shoe items. He used it. He loved it. Papa wasn't ashamed of my shop skills. I never even knew it.

"Yes, but how did the shoebox find its way into our house?" Sara inquired, always trying to fit the pieces together before they were given.

"After Papa passed away, I went to the house, peered under the bed, and it was still there, asking me to take it. It was as though part of Papa's spirit was somehow still in that box. Maybe because it was the only thing that I had ever made in my entire life, and he knew that it would be my last," I said, missing Papa deeply, trying to cover the quiver in my voice. But Sara always listened to everything spoken and unspoken, particularly the unspoken. Reaching for my hand, she looked at me, pouring her warm, steadfast love into my saddened eyes, giving me strength when I needed it the most.

"Well, at least you didn't have to wear what you made like I had to do in seventh grade," she said and grimaced, remembering the trouble that she had in her shop-like class, her home ec class. It was her first and only handstitched garment, a plaid pinkish skirt that was slightly longer on one side than the other. "My mother beamed with pride, thinking that the skirt was wonderful, delighted that I had done something inside instead of climbing trees and wandering at all hours outside on my bike. Of course, she insisted that I wear it to school as though it were a badge signifying 'girly.' It was horrible; the kids looked at me as if I had fallen out of an interstellar home economic class. I wore it one time then threw it away unbeknownst to my mother. Receiving a D in the course, I guess my hands weren't made to make things either." Sara sighed, acknowledging that now re-attaching buttons on shirts was the extent of her sewing.

"Did you also burn the food that you attempted to make in home ec?" I asked her lovingly, knowing how she hated to cook, thinking that maybe it all started back in seventh grade. She didn't reply, but I knew that I needed to go no further, so I retreated. It was my turn to reach for a hand, one that didn't want to sew or cook. I didn't care. All I needed was one that loved me.

But those hands could play the piano, and Sara sat down, softly playing some of her favorite songs.

"Get your guitar so we can try and harmonize some Christmas carols," Sara piped, wanting to get her mind off the dreaded day that was fast approaching. "School is going to be so difficult, the long hours, the kids, the 'gang want-to-bes.'"

I tried to reassure her that everything would be fine. I couldn't help but laugh, knowing that my wife was probably the only person on the face of the earth who practiced Christmas carols in August.

"Sara, you do this every fall, every year. Look at me. After my open-heart surgery I was out for three months, and everything was just as I left it. Just a new class with new kids, and that is just what you will be looking at. Your energy level and body will readjust just like mine have. Besides, your legs and chest are smooth, undefiled, unlike mine. About the

Christmas carols. Let me tell you when I played carols as a boy ... at the appropriate time, Christmas. I was thirteen years old, standing on a cold street corner. But all I could feel were my puckered lips against the metal mouthpiece of my cornet. I was a musical soldier for the Salvation Army, making beautiful music for my people, transforming my impoverished barrio corner into a corner of hope. The faces of my people told it all. They stopped, listened, and forgot. For a few minutes their hunger, cold, and tattered existence didn't matter. I took them back to an easier time, giving them something that mattered––a renewed spirit. I hoped that they would pass it along."

Thinking back about Christmas made me shiver deep inside, knowing that the boy of thirteen who played his cornet on the street corner helping fill the Salvation Army's clanging bucket was nowhere to be found. Too much had happened, too quickly. That young cornet player had vanished without a trace. I had little chance of ever finding him again.

Do it Right the First Time

The first day of school had arrived for my reluctant wife. Sara deliberately challenged it every step of the way. Routine was Sara's middle name, believing that it allowed her to get things done whether or not there was enough time to do it. Often this caused her to be late, and this morning was no exception. Nature was her panacea, and she embraced it as soon as she woke up. Her daily power walk started at five forty-five each morning while she was in a trance-like state. Functioning on cruise control, she made her way around the golf course that was home to numerous birds and a well-groomed lake that reflected the squinting sunrise as it rose. A numbing shower followed, and the countdown began. Suddenly every minute counted. Making it to school on time suddenly mattered.

As though pulled out of my dream by a frantic yank, I abruptly awoke with the crashing sound of Sara's war cry, "I can't find my car keys; they aren't anywhere. Did you take them? Have you seen them?"

I knew full well that she had to find them quickly. So with my logical, sleepy reasoning, I abruptly answered, "Where did you leave them last?"

That seemed to be what she needed to hear, just a bit of rational thought, and with that prodding, she hesitated, reached in the basket on the kitchen counter, and found them, much to her chagrin. After what seemed only moments, I was reawakened by a chorus of garage openers as though they waited for a specific time each morning before beginning their performance. Waking up in this fashion always unnerved me, taking years off of my life; I was sure of it. With the sound of the car's engine droning in the background, I eventually floated back to sleep.

After the performance, the phone refused to stop ringing. It was my secretary informing me of a mandatory meeting in one hour that I was expected to attend. Time usually wasn't a factor for me in planning my day because I had more of it; I could pick and choose when and where. Thirty-five years with a Ph.D. should bring you some bargaining power, but not so this morning. It appeared that I'd lost a chunk of it.

My colleagues' eyes latched onto me like targets on a torpedo, all except Dr. Myers, who never really could look me straight in the face because he knew that I would object to whatever meager suggestion that he made. Also there was Dean Swelling who hated confronting me because she knew my raw anger. There was the time I put one professor in the hospital with a heart attack because he dared question me, doubting me at a faculty meeting. He never questioned me again, refusing to attend any meeting if I were present. Doubtful looks flashed the questions: had I returned too soon after my quintuple bypass surgery? Was I still able to juggle the lecturing, grading, and public appearances? Was I succumbing to my health? I could hear the silent questions as if I were reading an opening statement. I didn't want to disappoint them, so I pounced.

"No, I don't agree with that grant proposal; it isn't written correctly, and it will never get passed." I knew the proposal had been incorrectly written and researched. It reeked of incompetence. "Whoever wrote this didn't follow the established procedure for grants, didn't even bother to consult an experienced researcher, and is completely unaware that it is obviously flawed. This by any standard is an insult to this institution." The words just tumbled out of my mouth as eyes widened, almost popping out of their sockets, and nerves twitched. My blood pressure soared. My heart started to hurt. It wasn't worth it.

"Polo, would you at least hear the proposal out?" said a befuddled Dean, knowing full well that my approval was absolutely necessary for its passage.

"No, the proposal must be done the correct way or not at all," I announced. Abruptly getting up, I had heard enough and headed directly for my office. Once again I had clogged the wheels of possible progress, but it wasn't progress if it was incorrect, and this was. Once in my office, I turned toward the silhouetted window and peered out. Mrs. Miller, my seventh grade history teacher, peered back at me, which only made me more angry. I had a confrontation with her as well about incorrect facts, other factors that contributed to the Mexican American War. Mrs. Miller made statements regarding the Alamo that were so prejudiced, so Anglo. When I opened up her prejudice, she shut me down and refused to listen to what I had to say. That day after school I went home and pestered Mama about what really happened in the Mexican War, and she pieced together a different type of quilt than the one that had been presented in class. There were two sides to the war, not just the white man's view. But I owe Mrs. Miller an eternal debt of gratitude for allowing the proud Mexican in me to question and ask why, hoping that after class she confronted her own prejudices. A soft distant knock disrupted my thoughts, and I was brought back to the present time by a softer, shyer, voice than Mrs. Miller's. It was concerned about my well-being.

"Polo, are you all right?" I barely heard the quivering voice ask, yet it was hardly waiting for my reply. The doubtfulness continued, "May I come in?" The concerned voice belonged to Ulna, an equivalent of myself in female form––proud, Mexican, and equally demanding on herself and others.

"You need to take it easy; it is only a faculty meeting, nothing worth getting sick about," Ulna slowly stated. "The other professors who attended the meeting are hiding in their offices behind locked doors afraid that you are going to barge in demanding answers to unanswerable questions. Why do you have to lash out at people that way? Why can't you just get your point across in a tactful way?" Ulna prodded, wanting reflection yet knew there would be none.

"You and I, we represent thoroughness and research."

"The rest need to value thoroughness as well, regardless of the issue or project." I didn't need a response. "We have worked too hard to have others pass off our ignorance or incorrectness as part of our cultural drawback. We need to be better than our Anglo counterparts. Ulna, remember how hard you had to fight when you were back in school just to make the Anglos realize that you could compete on their level and way beyond, but you had to prove it?" I stared into her eyes, well aware that I was about to lose it again. My face was drained and then suddenly I could hear Mrs. Dowell, my middle-school language teacher, calling off the students who had made the honor roll. Anglos: Adam White, Sam Sheppard, Susan Hickel, Meg Ryan, Mathew Greg. I felt the resentment and rage rise deep within me. From that moment on, I was determined that the next time she reeled off the names, mine would be one of the first. It was, much to the disgust of the others who considered the honor roll their domain and theirs alone.

"Ulna, it is just like what happened back in middle school," I said, telling her about Mrs. Dowell and the sacred honor roll. "We had to prove ourselves then, and we have to today. Nothing has changed, only the school." I sighed, completely worn out by the morning's events.

"Polo, you have more than proven yourself many times over. You are not thirteen years old anymore, and that hard-earned, well-deserved diploma on your wall, the one with doctor on it, says it all," Ulna stubbornly replied, choking on unleashed tears, all the while wanting desperately to reach me.

"But don't you see, Ulna. The others don't care how the grant is put together, but I do. I care. When you do something, anything of value, it must be done the right way the first time, or don't do it." After finishing this sentence, I could hear Mama's voice rattling, "You are my little soldier," and that just added more fuel to the smoldering fire that was inside me. Grabbing my cane and gripping it tightly, I hobbled nervously over to the window. "It reminds me of the time when I was in eighth grade. I wanted so desperately to go to Austin with the band to compete with other bands from other middle schools, but I didn't have the full uniform. I lacked the off-white leather loafers that were just too expensive for Mama to buy. The other trumpet players in my section seemed mildly concerned, yet it turns out they were secretly glad because that meant that I wouldn't be able to do the solo. But Mrs. Miller, my music teacher at the Salvation Army, just happened to find a pair of loafers that fit me even though I was sure that she had bought them. So I went to the competition and won, much to the shock of the Anglos. It was drummed into me that rules have to be followed exactly; details matter, even your shoes. Everything has to be done the way it should be done." I finished my thought, turned, and watched Ulna's inner feelings gush.

"Polo, it's all right. We will make the changes," Ulna said softly, hugging me like a young girl trying to comfort a frightened, thrashing bird that was trying to free itself from its entanglement.

I motioned Ulna over to one of the well-sat-on chairs in front of my unkempt desk bulging with heavily detailed reports, half-filled-in calendar appointments, scribbled memos on backs of torn-open envelopes, and books, all kinds of books from Statistics to The Latest Learning Theories in Learning Cognition, which lay in open cardboard boxes that begged to be pulled out and placed in a more appreciated spot, like the mahogany bookcase beside my window.

"Please excuse the mess, Ulna. I just haven't had a chance to put things in their proper place due to my absence. But this new office really gives me more room, for more books, and perhaps a few more pictures," I said hurriedly, forcing my voice to be calm.

"What's this? I don't ever remember seeing it before," Ulna asked curiously while reaching into a dimly-lit corner, removing a tarnished frame that held a family photo of the seven of us with Mama and Papa at the beach. I could almost hear the click of the camera while straining, listening to the cry of the pelicans in the background.

"It was one of those warm, summer days and the brown pelicans swished and swooped overhead as precise in their formations as trained ballet dancers, giving no heed to the gaping onlookers. But unlike the experienced pelicans, Mama watched over us and directed our every move because nobody knew how to swim except Papa, who couldn't have been more unconcerned. We had to be content with sitting in knee-deep water pretending that we were deep-sea adventurers. But I felt so carefree, knowing that Mama was there to watch over us and never left even for a moment."

"You do look happy; just look at the way you are smiling and hugging Aylvia and torturing Tito," Ulna said, looking truly amused, because she never imagined that I could be so carefree, worry free. "If this is you, where did you disappear to?" she asked, scrunching up her face.

"When we were together as a family, Ulna, everything made so much sense; all the pieces fit so well together. There were many hands to hold and hearts that truly cared, hearts that demanded safety. There was a sense of oneness among us. As a family we were powerful and joyful. Papa fueled our curiosity by taking us to different places and allowing us to wonder."

"Can you imagine taking your family to a butter factory?" I continued, well aware that Ulna also had that faraway look in her eye. "One Saturday morning while we were munching on tortillas and melted butter, Papa held up the blue crowned butter package and asked if we wanted to see how it was made. Quicker than you could finish a tortilla, we were on our way to the Falfurrias Butter Factory, which was about two hours away. Once we found the factory, I remember thinking that it didn't look like much from the outside, yet once we entered it was quite a different story. Before our very eyes there were numerous vats of creamy milk being churned into butter, and we were treated to samples of the finely-tuned mixture. It had to be done according to exact proportions, Ulna. The exciting part for me was that I discovered that there is more to a finished product than meets the eye; it's how precisely it is made."

As I finished my sentence, I turned my head away from Ulna and could still see Papa, Mama, and my brothers and sisters piled in the old Chevy delighted with our adventure, realizing that Papa wanted us to know what lay behind that fancy name, Falfurrias.

"So, if you got a lot of enjoyment out of doing simple things when you were younger, why have you changed so completely, finding so little enjoyment in anything now?" Ulna asked quizzically while shuffling slightly, determined to penetrate the shell that protected my childhood contentment.

"There is nothing simple about my life anymore. Nothing is the way that it needs to be. Everything and everyone only takes from me, only wanting what I can provide for them," I replied abruptly while pressing my fingertips against the coolness of the window pane, noticing how lovely the deep lavender tulip tree was that quietly hovered by my window, just wanting to be seen. It reminded me of the movie The Secret Garden. "Ulna, did you ever see it as a youngster?" I visualized the nine of us huddled together at a drive-in movie theater in Papa's old fifty Ford, clutching bags of homemade popcorn, noting every minute detail about a lush, hidden garden that lay in front of us. It tempted us to enter while we gazed with wide eyes in wonderment at the even wider, over-sized screen.

"That movie was by all means a classic," Ulna answered, having also recalled that moment of wonder when she was younger. "The ending was unbelievable, when the crippled boy walked toward her; you just had to hold your breath, hoping that he would make it. Unfolding right before your eyes, it was just so overpowering, all of the emotion that was between the children."

"We never had the chance to see the ending of the movie when we were at the drive-in," I thoughtfully replied. "Tito, who was about five at the time, got very sick, and Mama told us that we had to leave immediately; I can still hear the quiver that was in her voice, so with one last long look, we re-directed all of our energy into getting home. Suddenly that was all that mattered. Ulna, I will never forget the look on Tito's face when we left the movie: one of relief mixed with sadness knowing that he had prevented us from seeing the ending. That reminds me, Ulna, go look in that cardboard box behind the one marked 'odds and ends' over there; the one with the torn-open top."

"This one? It seems so light compared to the other over-stuffed boxes that are scattered around it," Ulna stated as her curiosity got the best of her. Reaching in she pulled out a worn thin white envelope with broken edges. A ticket slipped out. Quickly turning it over, she noticed it was a pass to the movie The Secret Garden, but it was forty years old. "I hope you don't have plans to go to the movie today."

"Ulna, that ticket is historical. For a very long time Tito felt very guilty about getting sick the one time that Papa could afford to take all nine of us to the movies. So on the morning that I left for college, Tito carefully slipped this movie ticket into my hand. No words were needed. I knew there would be a huge void in his life now that his big brother would no longer be there to lovingly harass him. That ticket says more than any conversation in any room."

"I never realized how close you were to your brothers and sisters," said Ulna, wishing that she had more time to linger. She had an appointment with a reluctant student in a few minutes and needed to hurry. "Polo, I'm meeting with a graduate student shortly and ..."

"Enough said," I answered as I motioned her to the door, feeling relieved that I could now be alone. But at the same time I felt a bit calmer from sharing. Funny how things turn out. It took my anger to allow time for us to talk. Usually it was hello, goodbye, or how is it going as I passed her, trying to get to my class while carrying a bulging briefcase in one hand, grasping my cane with the other, and steering myself, making sure that I didn't stumble on anything that lay unnoticed in my path. But I wasn't at all sure that I wanted to have any more unexpected conversations; it was just so hard to express in words what I felt. I was exhausted.

Peering at my desk that was strewn with family photos, I spied several pictures that had never enjoyed the dignity of being framed. Nestled in between two dignified pictures was a framed photograph, a close-up of Mama's face. Hearing a faint whisper, I leaned closer and heard it quite clearly like always. "You are my little solider," but this time it was as if she knew that I was doubting myself, my life, and everyone and everything that was important to me. I didn't care. Slowly and with great effort I turned the picture around so that I wasn't able to see her face.

"I am not your little soldier, nor do I want to be." But as soon as I uttered the words, I felt an overwhelming, empty sadness. A welling tear weaved a wet path down my quivering cheek.

THE TASTE OF WORK

Watching Sara feed her cats, I noted with interest how she hurriedly prepared the combined mixture of moistened and dry food, spreading it on the paper plate so that it could be sniffed and explored by her bundles of fur. After the cats came the birds. Our birds were lucky. They had feeding options: a wooden birdhouse with a teetering roof and clinging balconies or a more reserved cylindrical tube with openings along the outside that allowed the birds a sure footing. Migrating feathered visitors from Mexico, mockingbirds, chickadees, and even ducks swooped in for their share, not wanting to be left out. Listening to them squawk and coo as they flickered back and forth from tree to tree, I applauded as if watching a seasonal orchestrated performance.

"You know there is a real knack to feeding the birds." Sara's grin filled her determined face. "All you need is birdseed, a feeder, and some time, but not necessarily in that order." With her carefree nature getting the best of her, she turned her head ever so slightly to see if I had been paying attention and laughed, a weekend kind of laugh.

"Why do the most insignificant things delight you so?" I asked, wishing that I could find just a sliver of happiness in anything.

"Listen to the rhythm and tone of their chirping," she softly said. Closing her eyes, she was swept away with its simplicity and wanted me to relax and enjoy the wonder. I couldn't. When I did close my eyes, I didn't hear chirping but a raspy voice from my distant past urging me to continue unloading.

"You need to put your back into it. You will never be able to get this seed off the truck unless you speed it up. Concentrate on what you are doing." The words belonged to Mr. Perch, my first real employer, who helped mold my work ethic. I shuddered, opening my eyes and quickly realizing that the birdseed had triggered the thought of being back at Mr. Perch's feed and seed store. It was a tight-fitting store with barely enough space for the long, rectangular display windows, which were stuffed with heavy bags of cattle feed, bird seed, and chicken feed. My job was to keep the display window creatively maintained by hauling over-stuffed bags from one corner to the other. Because the clinging cash register was music to Mr. Perch's ears, I easily learned how to add up the charges and get a total. It was numbers, all math, which was one of my best subjects. But it was on that one particular day when I learned what blisters were. The weekly train had just come in, loaded down with enormous bags of cattle feed that needed to be unloaded into Mr. Perch's awaiting truck. I didn't think it would be that difficult; I was very wrong. After only tossing a few bags into the truck, muscles in my back were aching in places that I never knew existed. The bags had rubbed holes through the thin cloth of my gloves, leaving behind raw blisters that only added to my agony.

"Mr. Perch, sir, could I rest a bit? I have already unloaded ten bags," I heard myself ask, although I didn't know why since you couldn't rest until the work was finished.

"Polo, you need to get this train car emptied before dusk or I will have to get someone else to do it," said Mr. Perch, knowing that to question my ability was all that I needed to continue, and I did until I saw the dirty, pale brown walls of the train car observing me, surprised that I hadn't collapsed from sheer exhaustion. But my legs were protesting as I slowly hoisted the last bag of grain onto Mr. Perch's very loaded down truck. He smiled his special smile that acknowledged a job well done. He knew that he would make a man out of the exhausted boy who sat quietly beside him.

I felt a soft kick on my left sneaker that rapidly brought me back to the present, and refocusing, I could feel Sara's silent questions.

"The smell of the birdseed jolted me back to my past when I worked for Mr. Perch at his Bird and Seed store," I replied, deciding to share with Sara. "It was the very same odor that filled my nostrils every day during the summer of my eighth grade. But I still remember how lucky I felt to be able to get a job at all, especially one where I would be able to build up my muscles while getting paid. Mr. Perch was of slight stature and weight; however, he made up for it with wit and intelligence. Being one of Papa's good friends and a member of our Methodist church, he seemed to be a logical choice when I started searching for a summer job. He agreed to hire me for a few dollars a week, but more importantly, he would provide me with invaluable job skills, like an aching back, which I got every day. The money wasn't important to me; it was just being around the man, who had a unique way of fine-tuning his shop and his employees by reciting his never-ending motto of 'There is no time to rest when there is work to do.' On my very first day of work, I was greeted by a gnarled, withered hand that belonged to the warmest pair of brown eyes that I had ever seen, quickly putting me at ease. That first gnarled handshake was the beginning of a close relationship based on respect and admiration. The deformed hands belonged to Clifford, a very capable high-school graduate who was Mr. Perch's number one employee, in fact the only one. I learned many things from Clifford, yet the most valuable thing was something that he didn't even teach me: to cherish the little things like my two strong, healthy hands. Because of a bout of childhood cystic-fibrosis, Clifford had tightly-closed fists. But his mangled fists only spurred him on, making him fight harder. When it came to cleaning the floor, his twisted hands would quiver and shake as he spread handfuls of pungent sawdust from one end of the floor to the other. This was Mr. Perch's method of sanitizing anything and everything in the store. When Clifford tried to sweep the sawdust up, his hands refused to cooperate, so my able hands helped. He couldn't take his eyes off my hands. Part of me wished I could have given them to him."

Sara reached down and grabbed one of my able hands.

"Yes, hands can say a lot about a person," quipped Sara, remembering when just yesterday she had seen a group of hands that had been on an outing at Luby's, a favorite in-town restaurant with home-cooked meals.

"While I was ordering real food (not frozen) for us at Luby's, I couldn't help but notice a group of five elderly people, two attached pairs, and one single man. As they trudged carefully toward the entrance, the couples instinctively grabbed each other's hands, and the man followed suit as though he were also holding a hand. As he shuffled along, one of the other ladies turned around and saw his outstretched hand and grabbed it. It was such a compassionate moment of hands. After witnessing that, I just wanted to get home and reach for your hand, knowing that it would reach for mine as well."

It was moments like this that reconfirmed why I decided to re-marry, even though I had sworn to myself on countless occasions that I never would again. But here I was with someone who was perfectly happy listening to vocal conversations between the birds and observing people's hands. Oh, what I would give to linger down her path of contentment for a moment or two.

Suddenly Sara's hand became restless as she blurted out, "Why do they have to mow the golf course on Saturday morning right in front of our patio where there isn't any grass?" Right at that instant about twenty yards away, a prairie dog poked its head out of its burrow and nodded as though it totally agreed, looking like it had been rudely interrupted from its Saturday morning nap. As I followed the mower with my eyes, all I could think of was the time when Papa, Samuel, and I went to Mr. Trim's house to cut his lawn and carefully manicure the edges of the grass around the circular sidewalk. The job was never finished until Mr. Trim popped his head out and gave us the awaited nod of approval.

"Sara, did you ever help your father mow your yard?" I asked her, trying to get her mind off the aggravating hum of the mower, which was slowly decreasing in volume.

"No, I can't say that I ever did help with the grass, but I did shovel snow in the winter, earning up to forty dollars a driveway, which seemed a tremendous amount of money at the time. Mr. Goeben, strutting with a colored silk ascot, bringing out the robin egg blue color of his eighty-year-old eyes, was my snow-shoveling benefactor who lived across the street. Trying in vain to provide cultural activities for a gangly group of twelve-year-olds, Mr. Goeben took us to the ballet and opera, determined that we would be exposed to something other than climbing trees and building tree forts. His generous nature seemed to irritate his wife and maid, who didn't like children and were not used to the yelling, the constant need to be entertained. Four twelve-year-olds who would much rather be outside than in. When I shoveled his driveway, his wife and maid were delighted, knowing that they didn't have to show me how to shovel. But his wife did listen and watch like a hawk when her husband paid me. Often Mr. Goeben would give me a hundred dollars just because he could, knowing that I wasn't expecting it." Sara paused as she recalled a passionate time of childhood, an endless time of tree-tops, missions in the woods, and ice skating on the snow-topped lake behind Mr. Goeben's house. "The skating was done under the watchful eye of Mara, the black maid, who learned to like us because she had to."

"Sara, I bet you think that I have never felt the handle of a snow shovel. Well, I have, because once on a quick trip to see a Navy football game in Boulder, Colorado, my car got stuck in a fifty car pile-up on the highway. An unexpected blizzard caused the best of eyes to be sightless. Quickly I became a very resourceful snow shoveler. But getting back to the grass ..." I paused.

"Why, do you want me to earn extra money by mowing yards here at the club on weekends?" Sara said, scrunching up her face, hoping to get a chuckle out of me.

"Actually that isn't such a bad idea," I quickly replied. "No, it's just that the freshly-cut grass reminded me of the time when I helped Papa mow the yard of his employer, Mr. Trim, who was the parts manager at Best Motors where Papa was employed as a mechanic during the day and at night; he single-handily ran the dreaded wrecker service during the graveyard shift. Mr. Trim was a nice enough guy, but he always seemed to treat my Papa differently somehow, and it wasn't until that day that I helped mow his lawn before I finally figured out why. On this one Saturday, Samuel and I decided to surprise Papa and accompany him on his Saturday yard duty, helping him out by providing some much-needed muscle-power and teenage stamina, which he certainly appreciated. Papa was funny. I think he would have enjoyed being with Samuel and me on a Saturday just as much if we hadn't lifted a finger to help him, but that was not our way. What we accomplished, we did together with family pride. It meant a lot to us. Once we arrived, you could tell that Mr. Trim led a comfortable existence; his large yard enclosed a two-story brick home with all of the trimmings, including three-sided outdoor lanterns, a tiled walkway, a mailbox that seemed proud of its own gold-lettered numbers, and trees, lots of them, pecan, peach, and oak. I just remember looking up and seeing only patches of sky instead of solid blue, and a coolness that was ushered in when a breeze brushed across the yard. It didn't remain cool for long particularly after we had mowed, cut, and bagged debris, which took nearly four hours. With our thirst commanding attention, I remember that we requested water, which was brought out to us in paper cups, and never for a moment was there any indication that we were welcome to enter the house. While we were gulping the water, Mr. Trim's kids peered at us behind the closed window blinds, watched closely, and finally came outside. All they seemed to be concerned about was the heat, how we were cutting the grass, and why we had to help our father work. Then I heard it, a hushed whisper, "They're Mexicans." I felt awful. It was the way the little girl said it, the tone that she used. It sounded so terrible, as though we were something dreaded like a fungus or some other type of creeping crud. It was the first time that I felt uncomfortable about being who I was, wishing for the moment that I had blue eyes and blond hair, but only for a moment. Suddenly I realized there was much more going on here. Mr. Trim gave the orders, and Papa followed them. The pieces began to merge slowly like assorted chunks of broken ice meandering downstream on a thawing, spring-like winter day. I finally comprehended what Mama always said. Education matters, actually makes a person who he is or who he isn't. If Papa hadn't dropped out of school in the third grade, maybe Mr. Trim would be the one cutting his lawn just the way he liked it instead of the other way around. Without a moment's hesitation, I made a powerful promise to myself, that whatever it took I would get an education and would be the one who made heads turn, especially blond heads, giving orders that would be followed, demanding results the first time, allowing no room for error. Little did I know at the time how this promise would seep into my life and define who I now am." I stopped talking, feeling a draining sensation, unable to loosen the grip of that hushed whisper.

"Is that why you go out of your way to be nice to Gibe, the yardman?" Sara questioned, realizing now why Gibe was always invited in for a Coke or Pepsi after cutting the grass. Feeling quite ashamed, she knew now why

Polo was never concerned with Gibe's appearance after mowing or how long he stayed, just that he was invited in. She, on the other hand, had only been aware of Gibe's grassy imprint on the cushions and how many scuff marks he left with his mud-clogged boots.

"Yes, now do you understand?" I asked as tears clung to my eyes, longing for her to realize that it is where a man has been that is important, not his appearance, wanting her to have the instinct to look beyond and ask why.

A promise of her own was then made, and the next time that Gibe cut the grass, Sara would make a valiant effort to ignore the dirt and grime and invite him in without being asked to do so.

Sara decided now it was time to talk about what had really been bothering her ever since yesterday.

"I found a repulsive letter at school with language that no seventh grader should even know exists let alone write about," she stated, still upset at the thought of that neatly-written letter of disturbing words that she had picked up by accident during a morning break between her second- and third-period classes.

"A shocking letter to you may not be shocking at all for the kids," I answered calmly, wondering why she was so horrified. "Don't you remember writing or saying forbidden words just because you wanted to? Has it been that long since you have been such a goody–goody, Sara?" I grinned at her sheepishly. "The kids are just trying to define who they are, especially in seventh grade; I know that I was; it is just part of the process in discovering what you believe and what your boundaries are. That's what makes growing up so exciting, trying different things, regardless if they are acceptable or not."

"I realize what you are trying to get at and, yes, when I was that age, I remember running up and down the stairs at Watkinson, the private school that I attended In West Hartford back in Connecticut, muttering every swear word that I had overheard the older boys use. The headmaster who overheard me was livid and shocked," recalled Sara. "I just liked the sounds of the forbidden words as they rolled out of my mouth and didn't really know what they meant. It wasn't that I wanted anyone to overhear me ..." She could still hear the agitated voice of Mr. Tenney, the headmaster, ranting and raving why proper young ladies did not swear.

"Well, he must have gotten through to you because you never cuss. Well, hardly ever," I replied, visualizing the conversation with the headmaster. "Did you talk back to him the way you do with me?"

"No, of course not. I was taught never to talk back to my elders, but you are not my elder; you are my husband, lucky you," she replied, pouting. "No, but this is different. The letter that I found was intentional, taking quite some time to write. It was chock full of sexual comments that were put together in such a way that mocked any type of meaningful relationship. It was disturbing because I knew that it and others were probably being passed all around the school where many curious but innocent students would read it." Sara slowly sighed as she dug her prodding sneaker deeper into the annoyed crabgrass. "It just doesn't make any sense," she continued. "With one hand they are pulling out lip gloss and mirrors, and with the other they are clutching onto crayons and wanting to color during any free time that they may have."

"So, I gather you are referring to the girls, but––" Not being allowed to finish, I let her banter on.

"The boys are just as guilty; their mouths are busy dropping sexual innuendos whenever they get the chance without understanding a word of them, while their hands are busy working their finger skateboards, constantly riveting the desk tops, tumbling over makeshift pencil ramps, flying into the air and ramming into whatever they hit."

"I know that you are very upset by this off-colored letter of sorts, but be thankful that the only thing that most of the girls and boys pull out of their pockets is lip gloss and finger skateboards, not knives and cigarettes, which came out of our pockets when we were in seventh grade," I said as a look of confusion passed over her face. "When I was growing up, especially at school, a knife in your pocket was a sure sign of survival, and in the barrio one had to expect the unexpected. I think maybe the teachers knew that we carried them, but maybe they were fearful themselves and too scared to take the knives away from us. Spontaneous searches were done on certain kids whose behavior was questionable, but items such as cigarettes were just passed to one another out of sight of the unsuspecting teacher. I'm not sure why the knives were never found. It was fortunate that I was responsible and never once was randomly inspected. They wouldn't have believed their eyes." Sara's lip quivered as she interrupted me.

"I can't believe that you carried a knife to school with you in your pocket. Your mama never suspected that you had one?" She paused, wondering how in the world a knife could go unnoticed in a well-mannered pant's pocket.

"No, never, but let me tell you about that day, that terrifying day when I was so thankful that I did have my trusty knife. I can still feel the coolness of the raw steel handle of my pocket knife, noting every curve and nick of the cracked lacquer that encased the three-inch blade. Trembling, my fingers ached from holding the knife so tightly, waiting for that moment, the moment of necessity, which was now. It had all started innocently enough when Tomas, one of my good buddies, asked me if I wanted to go to Soto's, a local fast-food drive-in with his girlfriend, her sister, and him. Well, who wouldn't want to go, especially since Tomas had his own car and a great-looking girlfriend? With any luck the sister, Paula, would probably be great looking as well. As it turned out, she was. The four of us were busily munching on burgers, thinking of clever things to say when suddenly a loud muffler puffing smoke pulled up beside our car. Before I knew it, cussing filled the air, and all kinds of hand signs were being directed at me, coupled with dagger stares and leering shouts of 'Wait until school.' That was it, and then the car peeled off, leaving all of us quite perplexed, especially me, until I looked at Paula. Her unmistakable mumble rang in my ears as I stared at her in complete and utter disbelief.

"'That was my boyfriend, Chulo, better known as 'the crooked one.'

"Instantly Paula's great looks vanished, and the burger lost all of its flavor. But it was only Saturday afternoon, which gave me some time to pull myself together. Before I knew it, Monday morning stared at me in the face, along with Chulo and his cronies, who had surrounded me, resembling a pack of wild dogs with their heads held high in the wind, sniffing, just waiting for the signal, any sign to attack. I recognized Chulo instantly because it was the same Chulo who had wanted me to join his gang of terrorizing dropouts about a year earlier when I was in seventh grade. At the time I had seriously considered it because all of the kids seemed to look up to him so much, but later I learned that everyone was just terrified of him. Luckily I decided against joining his group, which is probably the main reason why I didn't end up as a seventh-grade convict."

"Well, what happened to that terrorized kid? What did you do?" Sara asked as a wildness clouded her face.

"Just when I thought that I was going to be breakfast for the dogs, I heard these crunching footsteps beside me. Turning around and to my amazement, there was Sam, the Crusher, a burly football jock who sneeringly said to Chulo, 'You will have to go through me to get to Pato.' After Crusher uttered those life-saving words, I quivered as the vibration of those eleven words ran up and down my spine."

"Wait, Pato was your nickname, but what did it mean again?" questioned Sara.

"Duck," I said, continuing. "Following Crusher were other members of the football team who trailed after him like kittens chasing a bug, and all of them were big, muscular, and begging for a fight. It was as if there had been a bit of divine intervention. Chulo balked and backed down, the circle faded away, and I loosened my grip on my knife, thankful that I didn't have to use it. I don't even know if I could have used it, to tell you the truth." I wondered what had become of Sam and the rest of the jocks.

"So that was the end of it; they left you alone after that?" queried Sara, trying to picture scrawny, undersized Pato next to the overstuffed football players and menacing bullies.

"Actually, no. When I turned around and headed toward the school, I heard a voice behind me say 'It's not over.' Glancing around, I saw one of the pack members motioning to me in a threatening way like movements John Wayne would make in one of his well-known movies. That same day after school I just happened to meet up with that very same tough guy, but this time packless. Startling him I said, 'Come on, show me what you have now, without your buddies around.' That did it. He just hemmed and hawed, shoving his hands in his pockets, mumbling that I had misunderstood him and wanted no trouble with me. That was the end of it."

"Security in numbers," Sara said and smiled, silently questioning how in the world Pato had made it out of his teenage years without being permanently damaged.

MY WORST FEAR

A sea of eyes were upon me. Surveying the anxious looks from the new university students, I noted with interest their body language as they propped themselves up in their chairs, listening intently to my opening remarks regarding my class and what was expected from them. The students seemed young, eager, and were furiously scribbling as I rambled on about what we would be doing and how we would be doing it. While concentrating on important concepts that I wanted the students to grasp, my dreaded fear violently exploded within me—a panic attack. Nauseous and gasping for air, I reached down, expecting to be grabbed by death, but instead I felt the solidness of the sturdy podium. Trying to steady myself, I quickly glanced down to see if I were still standing upright. I was. A sudden hush like the silence after a summer rain drenched the room. All that I was aware of was an outstretched arm that had wrapped itself around my wobbly waist, steering me to a nearby chair. Exhausted, I fell onto the rectangular square cushion. The class had abruptly ended itself without my permission. However, Albert, the alert Anglo student who was temporarily attached to me, did ask me for my permission.

"Dr. Saenz, would you allow me to help you back to your office?"

Being grateful for these simple, selfless words, I leaned heavily on Albert, not knowing whether or not we would even be able to make it to the office. However, Albert seemed confident putting me at ease and talking as though I had just finished a well-thought-out lecture.

"Doctor Saenz, I am really glad that I finally have the opportunity to meet you and take one of your classes," he quipped as he tightened his grip around my shoulders. It reminded me of the way the nurse cradled me after my heart surgery in post–op, escorting me to a semi-darkened room across from the operating room. His reassuring words just seemed to flow continually out of his well-meaning mouth. I was sure that he had probably taken Psychology 101, which had included what to do in this exact situation. Before I knew it, we somehow stumbled into my office in a fused piece.

"Albert," I managed to get out, "I will be fine; all that I need is just a little time to rest; then I will be as good as ever."

"Not to worry, Doctor Saenz. My next class isn't for another few hours, and I would be honored if you would let me stay here with you for a while," said Albert, sounding as though this closure had also been discussed in Psych 101. Albert reacted instinctively, reaching for the closest chair next to mine, not wanting me to feel embarrassed or awkward in any way. When I looked at him, really for the first time, I saw a young man of about twenty sporting a tan, with a closely-shaven head topped with ringlets of blondish curls and blue, curious eyes that jumped out at me, shouting respect.

"You know, this is really perfect timing because I have wanted to talk to you about my major ever since I found out that you are my advisor this year," Albert then said, making it seem as though we were meeting because of a scheduled appointment to discuss his course load and what he wanted to do. "This summer I had the unexpected opportunity to be a counselor for underprivileged kids at a nearby camp up in Greene, Texas, right near the Guadalupe River where everyone goes rafting. One of the counselors got ill, and they needed a replacement. I just happened to be in the area and volunteered but never expected the experience to change me and what I wanted to do."

By now Albert was beginning to get my mind off my panic attack, and I tapped into my professor mode. I was able to respond with my intellect, putting my ripping emotions aside for the moment. "In what way did it change you?" I replied, wondering what he was really trying to tell me.

"The kids," he answered, suddenly looking very intense, as though he had looked into the future and seen himself ten years from now. "I always thought that I wanted to teach older kids, more mature kids who grew up in suburbia, the kind of well-heeled kids who know college isn't a possibility but a given. But now having been around such deprived children, I have come to the startling realization that I want to teach younger kids, deprived kids who have little or no hope."

"That is quite a turn-around. It must have been some camp with some special kids," I softly said, thinking about my own camp experience.

Albert seemingly read my mind. "Have you ever been at a camp?"

"My camp experience, if you can call it that, was a one-time occasion, a visit. My sister, Tina, was enrolled at Camp Verde, a special summer camp for the challenged, the handicapped, or impaired," I wistfully said, recalling the day, the orange juice. "It was morning, and the eight of us met Tina in the mess hall where the table was encircled by juices. Five large containers were overflowing with grape, apple, cranberry, orange, and pineapple juice. Rarely did we have juice, and to have a choice was shocking. It was then that I realized why Tina loved camp so much. She could hardly wait for the first of June for camp to start. Every summer like clockwork Mama insisted that Tina go, hoping that she might return with sounds, any type of spoken communication that we could hear, but it never happened."

"I'm sorry, but I don't quite understand. Tina couldn't speak?" asked Albert.

"That's right. When Tina was about three she evidently saw something so disturbing that it kidnapped her voice, permanently. The kidnapper never revealed himself. Ever since that fateful day, she never uttered another word," I angrily answered, remembering all the times that I had prayed to God to take everything from me only to give Tina back her voice. My prayers were never answered. "But Camp Verde became an answer to my prayers. It was an oasis compared to the barrio. We were the underprivileged, the deprived kids just like the ones that affected you. I know what it is to be poor, to have nothing, only the barest of necessities. When I saw Tina's camp, I suddenly realized that there was so much that we didn't have: a swimming pool where you could actually swim in clean water and not worry about swallowing it, woods that had endless trails that you could actually hike on and not worry who was around the next corner, volleyball nets with leather balls that actually bounced, and the food, all kinds of food and actually not a single tortilla or taco. I will be forever grateful to Mama and Papa for sending Tina to that camp. It allowed her to experience a place where you didn't have to worry whether you would get enough to eat during the day or whether it was safe to play outside."

"I didn't know that you were so needy," Albert meekly said. "I just assumed that being a professor meant that you probably never had to struggle for anything, and——"

"Looks can be deceiving, can't they?" I interrupted him. "Education allowed me to slip off the shackles of my poverty." I paused for a moment, noticing that Albert had lost that careful composure of his, and his mouth was slightly ajar. "So you see the difference between us, don't you? As a boy, I lived my whole life with underprivileged kids; I was one. You visited them, and they opened your eyes so that you can see things differently."

"Maybe in a way we are both drawn to those who haven't had the best chances in life," Albert said, regaining his confidence. "There are so many of those needy kids right here at this college, in some of your classes. The Mexican border is right down the street. I am reminded of that every morning. If I don't get here early enough, all the available parking spaces are taken, jam-packed with cars toting Mexican license plates." Wincing slightly, I envisioned poor Albert trying to park his car, probably his father's leased BMW, as he inhaled the exhaust fumes that permeated the air from the annoying, broken-down mufflers. I realized that I must be feeling better if I was thinking about the parking lot. "And I," Albert said, jolting me out of the parking lot, "also want to make a difference with needy kids, but at the middle-school level where I think many kids just need direction."

Good for Albert, I thought; he is going beyond the BMW and his comfort zone.

Rearranging his thoughts, Albert continued, "Getting back to Tina, whatever became of her? How long did Tina go to that camp?"

"Until she no longer needed to go. Camp Verde helped Tina find her inner voice, a voice that lay undisturbed deep inside her. It finally woke up, giving her self-confidence and pride," I said, still amazed at how full Tina's life had become since her camping days. "When Tina was younger, she struggled almost every night trying to complete her homework, even

S.S. Simpson

with my help. I guess then I knew that her heart wasn't in it. Yet after a summer of camp, everything changed. Her self-confidence couldn't be bridled. Her creativity blossomed. Much to everyone's surprise, Tina got involved in sepia painting. Forty years ago it was a type of portrait painting that involved tracing black-and-white photographs with oil paints. When finished, they actually ended up looking like original portraits. Tina was an expert at it and studied each detail of the photo then applied different shades of oils, giving the portrait a lifelike quality. You really couldn't tell that it had once been a photograph. Watching her paint was a joy for me because she got lost in it, needing no one's help while creating such beauty so easily."

"Was Tina eventually able to own her own studio?" asked Albert, never realizing that oil paints could cover a black-and-white photograph.

"No, she did continue painting for some time, but then she developed other interests. Creating elegant dresses with patterns of colored sequins and fashionable tucks, Tina was able to master any design without anyone showing her how to do it," I said, remembering how all the neighborhood ladies wanted one of Tina's creations. "The most amazing thing that Tina ever made was her own son, Rito, who is a self-taught musician with his own band, playing the organ, trumpet, and guitar with ease and expertise. His group's musical debut happened one Sunday morning on the Johnny Canales program, a Hispanic show highlighting musical unknowns who wanted to become known. On that one Sunday, I was flipping channels on the TV, and there Rito was, but he never said a word about it until I brought it up. Rito also has a big band, a school band. He fine-tunes the musical talent of his high-school students and directs all musical performances. Can you imagine surrounding yourself with sound as an adult when you heard only a few sounds at home while growing up?"

"But why weren't there any sounds in his home?" asked Albert, not quite grasping what I had just said.

"Well, his father, Arturo, is a deaf mute and, of course, Tina never did regain her ability to speak. When their friends visited, all that could be heard was the faint clicking sound of finger movements." I paused. "But it just goes to show where there is determination, there is possibility."

"I guess that I am so used to my parents telling me what to do and how to do it that I can't even imagine what it would be like without their well-meaning instructions," said Albert, wondering how in the world Rito grew up, got educated, and found his independence, keeping music as his focus. "How did Tina and Arturo happen to meet? Were they childhood friends, or did Arturo happen to wander into the shop where Tina worked and become bewitched by one of her creations?"

"Neither," I replied, "but theirs is a real love story ... It all started innocently enough at a Quinceanera, which in our culture is celebrated when a young woman turns fifteen," I said as I heard the mariachis strumming their guitars softly in the distance. "It was a very rare occasion because Mama didn't believe in dancing and socializing in public, so I knew we wouldn't stay for long. I was in my Sunday best: a crisp, heavily-starched shirt complete with a rarely-worn red-striped tie, hand-shined black leather shoes (Samuel's hand-me-downs), and my only pair of good trousers that actually covered my ankles. Sitting all around me were my brothers and sisters, all seven of us. We were behaving publicly––talking half as loud as we normally did, facing in one direction in our seat instead of churning our necks around trying to see everything at once, and doing absolutely nothing that would embarrass Mama. But Tito, being six, was excused and could get away with doing almost anything. Continually demanding Mama's attention, he pulled at the hem of her dress that she was proudly wearing. It was one of Tina's creations. For a while Papa was doing what men did best, ignoring his wife and kids momentarily, pretending that he was once again a young man with no responsibility or cares. Since Spanish music stirred him, he searched for Mama's hand, cradled it, guiding her to the crowded dance floor. I was mesmerized because I had never seen Mama and Papa dance before; I could hardly believe my eyes. The guitars and serenading voices guided the dancing couples as they were whisked away back to younger years. When Mama returned to the table with tear-filled eyes, I thought maybe she was upset because Papa had stomped on her feet since they never went dancing. But her tears were not tears of pain. They were tears of joy. Suddenly the room hushed as a loving voice with a heavy Spanish accent announced on a microphone that Maria E. Rolando and her escort would be presented to her eager guests. Glancing around, if you didn't know any better, you could have mistaken it for a wedding party: on both sides of the couple were six girls dressed in white satin dresses, looking very grown up but biting their quivering lips. Next to each young lady was a dashing young Mexican boy dressed in a black tuxedo, puffing out his young chest like a cooing pigeon. Grownups around me seemed to miss a breath as Julio, her carefully-chosen escort, ushered Maria to a huge white chair laden with garlands of gardenias and white roses. After she was presented, then the fun really began. We were allowed to roam and dance for a bit after stuffing ourselves with assortments of meat like turkey, chicken, and sausage. We then dared one another to ask a girl to dance, any girl. That's when I noticed that this fellow couldn't keep his eyes off Tina. He was good-looking enough with a full head of wavy, brownish hair, which matched his dancing brown eyes, and a nose that fit well in his face. He didn't look athletic; rather he was pale and thin. As I happened to be turned around, I noticed his fingers moving in slight movements while he was admiring Tina. Much to my surprise, Tina's fingers were moving even quicker as her questioning eyes watched for answers. The longer I looked, I finally realized that they were signing and having quite a conversation unlike others who couldn't understand a word anyone was saying because the music was very loud. Before long this lanky fellow stood up, shyly walked over to our table, and sat down awkwardly in a nearby chair that Tina had pulled closer to hers. The rest just fell neatly into place ... slowly, with gaps here and there, and years later, fifteen to be exact, they were married, which didn't surprise anyone a bit, especially Mama."

"I guess time has a way of evening out the odds," stated Albert, repositioning himself in his chair by stretching out his long legs but remembering quickly that he was in a professor's office and quickly folding them back.

It was time that I redirected Albert's thoughts back to his studies, and I did.

"Getting back to your comments regarding what level you would like to teach," I continued, "were you saying that you might want to add additional classes to your schedule, especially those geared more toward middle school?"

"Well, yes, in a way, I guess, but I was thinking a bigger change, like transferring to another college in a different area so that I would be able to become more well-rounded, more independent, if you know what I mean," replied Albert, hoping that I might understand what he was really trying to uncover. "Doctor Saenz, did you ever get the urge to leave the Valley when you were younger to see what else was out there?" Albert asked as he respectfully waited for a much-needed answer from me.

"You mean, did I ever take risks, chances, and become a more interesting person?" I commented, knowing all too well those rushing feelings that could easily drown any other thought. "Being raised in the barrio, I knew that I didn't have much, but what I did have was a quick wit, a God-given ability to learn easily, and the good sense to know right from wrong. But the barrio made me who I am; it taught me how bad I could be and what might happen if I associated with the wrong type of kids. Mama never knew that side of me even existed, but there was this one time when I thought she would find out. I could still hear the voice of the license examiner as she peered into my eyes.

"'Are you here to get your driver's license, too?' She had just given my older sister, Avera, her written driving exam. Well, I didn't want to disappoint her, so I nodded my head, took it, passed it, and got my license. My buddies wanted to celebrate my good fortune since I was now a legal driver. They suggested that I borrow Papa's car just for a few hours and go sightseeing at the local pub, a beer and pool hangout. Before I knew it, we each had a beer in one hand, a pool stick in the other, and were concentrating on acting older, much older, which meant of course, more than one bottle of beer to a hand. Drinking beer wasn't anything new for any of us, but the quantity was, especially for my buddy Eddy. After a few beers, he was fast asleep, unconscious. We just stood there looking at one another. Our grown-up cover was blown. It was replaced by fear. No one knew what to do. All heads turned in my direction, assuming that I would have answers, but I didn't.

"'Polo, what should we do with Eddy, leave him here?' There was a throng of voices, a chorus of confusion. 'No,' I heard a grumpy voice from the back of the room say, 'you need to get your friend out of here; this is not a hotel.'

"If I took Eddy home, then his parents would call Mama and Papa. I would be grounded for life, but leaving him there wasn't an option. So as we visualized life sentences, a plan was conceived. Somehow we got Eddy into the backseat of Papa's old Ford, propped up like a limp noodle. As we neared Eddy's house, I eased the car up quietly, slowly, to Eddy's front yard. The lights were off, but the full, orange moon hung directly over us, watching, waiting for possible mistakes. There were none. Danny opened the rear car door. Everyone took an arm, leg, or head, and we carefully deposited him on the front lawn. That was a sleepless night, especially for me, because I kept waiting for the phone to ring, knowing that any minute my entire life as I knew it would change forever. But it never did."

"But how come you never became a bad kid and remained in the barrio?" asked Albert, trying hard to keep his mouth closed, not looking too shocked at what I said.

"Probably because Papa knew all the policemen in town. At night he was on call for the local wrecker service towing car parts that remained after accidents to Best Motors. One particular Anglo policeman, Smitty, always seemed to know where we were and what we were doing. When we got ourselves into trouble, he would call Papa to come and get me, knowing how hard Papa worked and how proud he was of me. Known for my responsibility and helpfulness, I guess poor Smitty thought it was unthinkable for me to be included with the rest of the thugs who would be dragged down to the courthouse in the dead of night. Papa thought discrimination might be a factor since my friends were poor, Mexican, and usually at the wrong place at the wrong time. Sometimes Smitty would harass us for being on the corner and blocking traffic then accuse us of stealing fruit from the nearby orchards if he found any on us. Mostly what we did was harmless, but I did learn from some of the ringleaders how to start a car without keys. Thinking back on it, Papa probably knew something that I didn't. When one of the Anglo football players got caught breaking into a business, he was escorted to jail and then within an hour was out with all charges mysteriously dropped. However, today that same football player is now a reputable doctor, so maybe his friends just dared him to do it. If he had been a Mexican ..." I stopped short, already making my point.

"But what made you want to achieve, to do something with your life?" Albert asked, wondering how in the world I became a professor with a background like mine.

"I had to fight and fight hard, especially at school, because I was poor and Mexican; I had to prove to everyone, mostly the other Anglos, that I was just as smart as they were, if not smarter." I recalled that ten-minute talk with my high-school counselor, Mrs. Gofar, which changed my life abruptly.

"Polo, I brought you in here today to talk to you about your class schedule," said Mrs. Gofar, looking quite concerned as she leafed through a packet of papers with my name on it. "From now on, you will be enrolled strictly in honor classes, taking all the advanced science and math classes that are available. No longer will you have the luxury of taking regular classes. Enough of your valuable time has been wasted. Your SAT test scores indicate that you should be in the top ten percent of your class. That is what I expect from you." Finishing, she flashed me one of her famous encouraging smiles, which caught me off guard. At that very instant, the barrio lost its controlling grip on me. Someone other than Mama believed in me, an Anglo. It was the controlled shove that I needed. It must have been a conspiracy because about that same time, Mr. Clearview, the principal, began to closely monitor my behavior, intervening, steering me toward the good kids with an ingenious plan. When the absentees had been counted in the office, I was assigned to accompany Mr. Clearview to search for those absentees, who happened to be my buddies. So the two of us rode around in his well-known car patrolling my neighborhood. By going house to house, the word got out that I was a turncoat and spy, and from then on those buddies didn't want anything to do with me. Then I had more than enough time to do my homework, to be a band officer, and to concentrate on school activities, especially dancing, escorting many of the chosen homecoming queens to proms. When graduation time came, my grades were what they should be, but my income was limited. I decided to take my basics, majoring in math and science at Pan Am, a junior college that was about thirty minutes away from home."

"Did you work while you were going to high school?" asked Albert, realizing it was probably way too obvious a question, and he shouldn't have asked it. The next question was equally as obvious, except to Albert. "How come you weren't eligible for a scholarship?"

"Back then there were scholarships, but only a few were available for minorities. Yes, I worked. I worked hard every summer that I can remember and also during the school year when I could. During my high-school years, one of Mama's church friends, Mr. Chico, who owned a dry-cleaning laundry business, hired me and taught me everything there is to know about clothes: how to coordinate and keep them spotless. Looking like he owned the neighborhood, Mr. Chico and I would deliver the crisply-pressed dry cleaning on hangers to the impressed customers. He was always giving me advice, impressing upon me how important it was to have one expensive, well-made suit that you could wear anywhere, anytime."

"So that is where you got your flair for dressing. Did you know that you are usually one of the opening topics of conversation on any given day? It is the way you dress. Your starched shirts, coordinated ties, and matching pants. You set yourself apart from the other professors who on a good day may match but usually are wrinkled and hurriedly put together."

"No, I wasn't aware of that, Albert," I said casually, looking at my tie. "But getting back to your previous question, when I was going to Pan Am, I worked as a PE coach at the local community center in Pharr, which was about halfway between college and home. I guess that is when I realized how much I enjoyed working with groups of children: playing basketball, baseball, tennis, and soccer."

"So that really was the start of your teaching career," commented Albert, who was clearly enjoying listening about my college days, taking the time leap back with me.

"I guess it could have been. But after attending classes for about a year and a half at Pan Am, things suddenly changed," I said. "One of my buddies heard about a pharmacists program being offered at the University of Houston. The requirements were advanced math and science credits, which I had. Making the opportunity sound even more interesting was the fact that there was some very affordable, low-rent housing available near the college: twenty-five dollars a month per student to share a multi-bedroomed home with an elderly, recently widowed live-in homeowner. Before I knew it I was carrying pharmacy books and living in a four-bedroom home with other college students who were from the Middle East: Lebanon, Syria, Iraq, and Iran. Only two hailed from Texas––Jimmy and I. It was an international household, and we learned to adjust to different foods, habits, and lifestyles. The house owner, Mrs. Whitsel, was herself a transplant from Louisiana. Her nurturing ways plugged the homesick gap with motherly advice. I will never forget that first Saturday when Mrs. Whitsel invited me to share a cup of coffee with her. As I took a big gulp, all I could taste was bourbon. My face must have been a dead giveaway, as she casually mentioned it was the Cajun way of drinking a proper cup of coffee. From then on, when I went home to visit, drinking coffee with Mama was never quite the same."

A chime clanged clearly in the distance.

"Oh my gosh, it's already time for my next class," Albert said, picking up his book sack, wishing that he didn't have to leave. Getting up he quickly added, "Doctor Saenz, thank you for taking your valuable time to talk with me. It helped me realize that it isn't too late for my dreams." He reached out his hand and met mine. I, in turn, was grateful that he was there for me when I desperately needed someone's help. I double-checked making sure he hadn't hidden any tufts of wings.

PAPA

After my panic attack at the university, I was less in control and more vulnerable. My panic attacks could surface at any time, any place not needing my permission. But worrying about it wouldn't change anything. I needed to block it. One sure way was to visit my family. I didn't have long to wait——the telephone rang, bringing a mouth-watering message: "Tina made her umbuellos." That was all that I needed to hear. I could taste one of those slow, batter-dipped tortillas loaded with cinnamon and butter. Preparing umbuellos was a tasty part of Mama's legacy that only Tina seemed to have mastered, having the desire, time, and patience. It was a real event when she fixed them, and I wanted Sara to taste them. The word spread like measles. Before I knew it, Tina's tiny house became a bustling eatery. When we were all together inhaling the umbuellos, it was as if Mama was right there with us. Sinking into a chair, I felt my uneasiness evaporate like steam from heated water. As Sara watched, my four sisters surrounded me as though I were a long-lost relative who had just been found. Amberina, the second oldest of the four, always wanted me to look perfect. That meant meticulously cutting the curls off the ends of my hair, trimming the pepper out of my beard, while she filled me in on happenings at her emotion-packed Pentecostal church. As my hair was pampered, Avera, my youngest sister, started to fill me in on her teacher problems, knowing that I had thirty-some years of teaching experience.

All the while, Aylvia, sister number three, draped her arms around me as if I were a window that needed covering, reminding me the most of Mama because of her warmth and genuine caring.

Listening to the conversation around me, I couldn't help but overhear Amberina say that she was thinking of getting back into the beauty salon business: styling and cutting hair. She put her thin hand on my shoulder.

"I miss it; the craft itself, the creativity, the conversation, all of it," said Amberina softly, rolling her moistened eyes toward me. Do you remember Austin ... ?"

How could I forget it? She was single, twenty-five, and Mama and Papa had decided that she needed to move her scissors and hair dryer somewhere other than their house. Her business needed a place to go. So she moved in with me and my young family, relocating her business. My neighbors were grateful, although my wife was not.

I slowly reached for her wandering hand and said, "Let's go outside and see how much the fig tree has grown." The word fig seemed to lighten her face when she looked down at me. It was as if she were ten again and getting ready to raid the fig tree before the others could find the sweet, brown, ripened fruit.

Feeling that it was now time for some brotherly guidance, we talked about what was really bothering her. As we stood under our childhood friend, things hadn't really changed all that much; I was still her older brother trying to fix things, plugging up any of life's occasional leaks. It was my obligation, as well as my choice because of Mama's last request: "Promise me that you will take care of your sisters and brothers, and Papa." As we reentered the house, I couldn't help but notice the way the ground had been carefully tilled beneath the olive tree and hedged around the vegetable garden leading to the side door. The house had been given a second chance. Tina and her husband, Arturo, had moved in and changed it. Papa used to live here.

Once inside, Papa was on my mind. I made myself go into the room—the room where everything unraveled in an instant. Sitting on the bed, I could still hear the voices, the confused sounds from Tina, shrieking on the telephone, trying her best to tell me what had happened but not really knowing herself.

All I remember was hearing something that sounded like blood. I knew something was very wrong. Although it didn't make sense to me, because Sara and I just saw Papa the day before when he devoured a plate of enchiladas loaded with beans and rice followed by his favorite, a piece of strawberry cheesecake. However, during lunch Papa had talked an awful lot about Mama's beans, rice, and the way he used to brush her long, thick, grayish hair, then wrapping it around her head in a stylish way. Suddenly I wished I had listened closer, hearing what he was really trying to say.

With Tina still shrieking, I remember hearing myself say "911." Dropping the phone I grabbed my car keys. I waited for what seemed like forever in a cold, dimly-lit room with seven other anxious faces, including Sara's. She had come to love the old man with his soft tender Mexican ways.

"He just wanted to know the date, and we never gave him one. Now he will never know," sobbed Sara, knowing she had taken something precious away from Papa. Why didn't we just settle on a date, she thought. She knew the answer: the fear of the future and becoming a Mrs.

Stubbornly all of us sat, waited, and agonized as Papa rested peacefully, unconscious on the sterile white hospital sheets in the next room.

The next statement was from the nurse. I wished that I could lock it out of my mind forever. She cowered slightly in front of us, whispering, "He doesn't have much time left." With that one sentence, reality left me; I wasn't aware of the others or what was happening around me. All I knew was that Papa needed me, but I needed him more. When the nurse finally nodded, that awaited nod permitting family visitors, I was the first to enter the dimly-lit room, giving anything to hear Papa say, "Why, there you are, son," but nothing was said, only the silence soaking in my tearful gasps.

I reached for Papa's sun-drenched hand and cried, "Papa, I need you. Don't leave me now. I can't keep the family together without you." But his hand didn't respond. Nothing did. I had never felt more alone than at that moment, and I sobbed on Papa's chest, wanting to feel his breath, the pounding of his chest. The coolness of the plastic tubes that were connected to Papa's nose was all that I felt, and I heard only the whirling hum of the respirator. My breakdown was uncontrollable but was snuffed out by Mama's little solider who knew he had to be strong for everyone else. My tears turned to rage, my whimpering melted into ice; everything froze; I didn't exist after that moment. One by one my sisters and brothers entered the sterile room, looking in horror at papa, frightened, trying to say something that mattered yet giving up because it didn't. When Sara walked into the room, I was standing, unable to connect with the Papa that was in front of me. She went to him, took his hand carefully, as though it were porcelain, and prayed the Lord's Prayer as she had never prayed it before.

When she finished praying for both of their souls, she slowly said to Papa, "Everything will be as it should," and promised to take care of his Polo forever, becoming a Mrs. on June 21. Weeping, she slowly got up and left, knowing I needed to be alone with Papa. After what seemed like an eternity, the words just started to tumble out of my mouth as though someone else were speaking them.

"Papa, I know that you need to go, and if that is what you want, then that is the way that it will be. The nurse just told me that she wants me to take you off the respirator, but, Papa, I won't do it that way; you need to show me somehow that you have decided to go and join Mama in heaven, by yourself, without anyone making you leave before you are ready to go. Please, Papa, I won't make that decision, so I am begging you that if you need to go with Mama, go now by yourself, and know that I will take care of the family, making sure that everything is done the way that you would have wanted. Know that I love you more than my life. I always have." I stopped, clutching Papa's hand as I spoke, feeling a movement, a slight bend of a finger. I whispered, "Papa, look for Mama; she is waiting for you. All you need to do is let go and go to her." After saying these words, I sensed someone gazing down at me. Instinctively I tilted my head back, saw Papa and Mama hand in hand, smiling, looking peaceful and complete. After a precious moment they vanished, leaving me very much alone because I knew he was gone. Now somehow I had to tell the others.

Startled, feeling a pair of strong hands gently rubbing my aching neck, I found myself twisted, halfway lying on Papa's bed in his bedroom, realizing that the agonizing news was already known; it had happened five years ago. Heaving a grateful sigh of relief, I turned and felt a warm kiss on my moist cheek.

"Polo, your sisters said that you were lying down, but you're trembling and sweating. What's the matter?" Sara asked but knew that something was very wrong when I didn't attempt to answer her.

"It's Papa, he's gone. He just died again in my arms the way he did five years ago at the hospital; now he's with Mama in heaven, but I miss him. I miss them both so much. I don't think I can go on this way, always hurting inside, always taking care of everyone else, never having any time." I paused, not wanting to continue. I had said enough, knowing I had said too much. Tears were streaking down Sara's cheeks. Holding me close to her, she calmed me in a way that only she could, stroking my cheeks and telling me that everything was going to be all right. Closing my eyes, I could feel Mama's gentle touch, caressing my cheeks in that same, unforgettable way.

"Polo, I am here for you, and I love you up to the sky and down again," Sara whispered lovingly, quoting the ten most powerful words that she knew. Her Mother whispered them to her as a little girl whenever she had felt helpless, desperate. The phrase had been passed down from one generation to the next, being taught to her mother from her Grandmother Simpson, who had a great fondness for teaching, painting, and the piano. Not only had Sara inherited her middle name but also her love for the piano, painting, and teaching, most of the time. But now she knew instinctively that she had to reach me no matter what.

Shaking, I grabbed her hand, feeling as though I had been pulled out of a stormy sea. Gulping for air, I suddenly felt safety beside me, my beloved Sara. Opening my eyes, I looked up and saw that determined look, knowing that there was enough inner strength for both of us.

"I don't want the others to see me this way," I softly said as I tried to shake the panic that had gripped me, leaving me nearly exhausted. "They won't understand; they have never seen me this way before; they will be——"

"Polo, you know your sisters. Once they start talking ... You probably haven't even been missed," Sara replied, trying to sound reassuring, although sudden hollers from the hall confirmed my fears.

"Where's Polo?" a persistent voice from around the corner shouted.

So, the hours trudged on, but always in the back of my mind I expected Papa to walk into the room at any moment and ask, as he always had, "Son, do we have time to go to Ross's because I don't have any more socks or undershirts?"

Just this once I wanted to answer him, and softly did, "Yes, Papa, I will take you to Ross's and buy you as many socks and underclothes that you think that you need." I hoped that he heard me, but all I heard was the throbbing beat of silence as it wrapped itself around me.

Suddenly I got up and heard, "Do you want any of Papa's socks and undershirts that are piled up in those tattered, cardboard boxes on the porch?"

"Yes, I'll take all of them," I replied, almost choking and quickly headed for the porch, knowing that Papa had heard me after all and answered me in his own way, the only way he could.

UNCONFIRMED

Time had passed, maybe too much time, since I had last seen him, but there he was in front of me. Tito, my younger brother, a confirmed bachelor of many years was ready to become "unconfirmed." He had somehow found Almita, the one who had flipped him over like an up-righted canoe that was once again ready for a long race downstream. Crisply buttoned to its top, his black and white tuxedo shouted with pride and framed Tito. He glowed. As the immediate family waited for the bride to make her entrance into the makeshift garden, complete with red and black Japanese lanterns that swung effortlessly in the billowing breeze, I noted with envy how truly happy and relaxed Tito was as he stood, eagerly waiting for his bride-to-be. He didn't have long to wait; Almita just seemed to appear, looking as though she were nearly swallowed in satin and lace. Her face was only slightly hidden with wisps of pearls that clung to a white-beaded headdress that lay softly nestled in her well-arranged hair. As Almita came into view, there was that moment, that hesitation of wonder, knowing that everything was about to change, never again to remain the same.

Thinking about how things change, I remembered my own day of becoming unconfirmed five years ago with my own canoe rightsider, Sara. On the early morning of our wedding, June 21, it was seasonably hot and too quiet. Longing to hear Sara's voice, I listened but couldn't. Her early morning wakeup service had malfunctioned. Sara had been abducted by her parents and extended family, including aunts and uncles who had traveled from California and Oklahoma to see her actually commit herself to someone, something. It was so shocking. No one had ever expected or considered it possible since she was forty-something. Those two unfamiliar words, "I do," were not part of her vocabulary.

The evening before whirled away much too quickly, with the wedding rehearsal and dinner going smoothly as planned and with only bits of hesitation here and there. Secretly I think Sara's father couldn't wait to be released of the burden of worry that he had shouldered diligently for forty some-odd years. Straightening my own shoulders just a little, I realized that they were looking forward to the extra load that was soon to be placed upon them.

When around my fellow professors, Sara had a tendency to be a bit timid, so we decided, well, really she decided to keep the wedding small yet very traditional, as her family had been firmly rooted in rich New England soil, although found itself transplanted to clay-weathered Texan soil. Keeping with tradition, the service would be held at the La Feria Methodist Church, a quaint, stained-glass faced church that had been in Sara's family for decades. As a little girl growing up on a farm, Sara's mother attended the very same church every Sunday with her Grandmother Simpson. It was at this very church that she became unconfirmed and married her Yankee husband, a preppie Yalie. He had been randomly stationed nearby as a training soldier while waiting for his orders to be shipped overseas. After a courtship of hooking worms and milking cows, the two opposites decided to make their brief time together permanent. Desperately wanting to be married before his orders forbade it, Sara's mother, who was a pre-med at Vassar, opted for her soldier and left her studies behind, saying "I do" within two days of his scheduled departure. As fate would have it, World War II came to an abrupt end, so he never went overseas, and his pre-med honey donned a nursing cap instead of a stethoscope.

Choosing a nursing cap as well, Meg, Sara's older sister and the maid of honor, now donned a pen as she embraced administrative hospital work. Not well versed in train carrying, Meg kept us in stitches as she practiced her unique style of carrying thirty feet of lacey satin, as her husband Mark provided head-bobbing encouragement. My younger brother, Tito, was my best man and couldn't believe that I would walk down another aisle laden with gardenias after fifteen years of utter chaos with my former wife.

Yet that was yesterday, and now I was ready for today, anxious to make Sara my coveted wife. Early was better, and I arrived very early at the Methodist Church with plenty of time for last-minute checks and rechecks. I confidently fiddled with my bowtie until I had it right, or at least until the mirror agreed with me. Feeling very coordinated and romantic in my three-quarter length tuxedo and tails, a prerequisite for Sara, I listened while strains of Mozart and Vavaldi were being fine-tuned by the much sought after violin and cello quartet. Strings were tightened and relaxed as the musicians practiced, knowing that their performance would make or break their established reputation. The wedding ceremony didn't start until five o'clock, but there seemed to be a heightened expectation as the hours nudged closer to the awaited time.

Brad, the newly-elected pastor of the church, eagerly confided in me, "Polo, you know how much this ceremony means to me, being my first official wedding as pastor of this church, don't you?" Hearing the questions beyond his question, I answered silently that it would be a flawless ceremony, although time proved me very wrong. As five o'clock peeped its head around the corner, Brad was parading up and down the uniform sidewalk in front of the entrance, marching with deliberate steps, his black crimson-lined robes billowing in the breeze like distress signals, hoping against hope that the bride would be arriving momentarily, but she didn't.

With darting looks of concern, Brad finally motioned me to form a two-man huddle and asked me pointedly, "Polo, do you think she is on her way?" This time I think he needed an answer, and so I gave him one.

"Brad, Sara will be here eventually. You know how brides tend to be, wanting to look perfect, flawless, on their wedding day with so many eyes on them, especially since her train is about as long as the aisle." I halfway smiled, although Brad didn't see the humor in my statement at all. You see, I wasn't too worried because I knew Sara; she was always late for everything, so I guess today was no exception. Glancing at my watch, I noticed that it was headed for six o'clock. By this time Jacob, Sara's younger brother, unconfirmed and forty-something as well, had carefully roped and re-roped off the parking area in front of the church with a golden braided rope, anticipating the limousine's grand entrance. Constantly patrolling this section, he too appeared a bit concerned, while he adjusted and readjusted the ropes as if he were expecting a stampeding herd of prize cattle. From the corner of the horizon, a recently polished, black limousine came puffing down the street looking as though it had just finished the race of its life. Like puppets on a string, people suddenly appeared from nowhere, crowding around the limousine, opening doors, laying out the defining red carpet, and breathing huge sighs of relief.

"More to the left, center the steeple, make sure to get the train," barked the photographer after a slight sigh sneaked out of him. It was not one of relief but one of agitation since he had been waiting over an hour for a glimpse of the bride-to-be in her elegant wedding dress. While lights from the camera were popping, Meg, Aunt Jane, Percy (Sara's father), and, of course, Sara couldn't wait to get out of the champagne-laden limousine, looking perplexed and alarmed. Edna, the mother of the bride, who had been busy reassuring me that her daughter would be here any minute, looked very relieved as her eyes welled up with tears, thankful that she didn't have to make up any more reasonable excuses why the limousine hadn't arrived.

Sara's father, who had previously done the wedding walk well, now had apparently become one complete step ahead of Sara because he had started with his left foot instead of his right one, not waiting for the pause in between steps. While he half-pulled her down the fragrant aisle, Sara somehow kept up, while Meg, who was attached to her train, held on for dear life. Percy's face said it all; things were not quite as right as they should be. His true emotions started to unfold since the dulling champagne that they had gulped in the limousine had started to wear off. One look at Sara confirmed it: she was ashen white and a nervous wreck. Approaching the altar trembling, she reached for my hand and began babbling:

"The limousine was late. The driver got lost and couldn't find the house, so father had to go and direct them from the main clubhouse." Sara mumbled nonstop as though she were on trial, trying to persuade a jury of her innocence.

Placing my hand on top of hers, I whispered to her softly, "Everything is fine, and I hadn't even considered leaving. Well, not for very long." I smiled, trying to reassure her because our vows were waiting patiently to be heard.

"Dearly beloved, we are gathered here today," Brad began, having gotten over his tiff about the late start, yet I still heard a tinge of exasperation in his voice as he continued with the vows. When I was asked the crucial question, to love and to hold until death do you part, I answered, "I do," without a moment's hesitation; however, when it was Sara's turn, there was an awkward silence that resonated off the organ bellows. I just looked at her and was sure she was going to faint or go raving down the aisle, claiming that she had made a terrible mistake. But, thank goodness, Brad had experience with first-time brides of forty-something and repeated the question. This time Sara squeaked out an "I do," instantly shattering the safety of yesterday, replacing it with uncertainty, a binding covenant witnessed by everyone she had ever loved, including her God. Everything had changed in less than a moment, never again returning to the comfortable past.

When the soloist, an opera wannabe, started her vocal translation of the Lord's Prayer, Sara actually released her knot-like grip on my hand and started to relax a little. While the violins wafted in and out, serenading the singer, a certain calmness reached her. Music was Sara's trigger for unwinding. Her piano practicing had become an active partner in our relationship. "Is she beginning to enjoy any of it?" I wondered out loud. As the service ended, all trails were supposed to lead to the country club where the reception was to be held, but ours took a brief detour. While readjusting ourselves in the limousine with our minds on us, we hardly noticed how the car bolted away from the curb doing an acrobatic u-turn in the middle of the street because Marcela, the capped, Mexican driver, suddenly realized she had started off in the wrong direction. No sooner had the wheels skidded across the pavement than an irritated siren shrieked its objection, pulling the limousine over, while Marcela muttered bits of altered Spanish under her breath. Being a lady cop, one might think that the law would have had some sentiment for our being newlyweds, yet that one factor really seemed to irritate her even more. First, Marcela had to verify her citizenship with all sorts of documentation, which she luckily had. Then finding no fault with the paperwork, the obnoxious policewoman yanked out her ticket-book and started writing furiously, determined to prevent us from being on time for our reception, which she accomplished. Upon arriving, we witnessed that Edna's painstaking plans for integrated table seating had vanished. Arriving early, a few guests, members of my extended family, had intentionally changed all the place settings so that integration was no longer a factor. By choosing not to sit with Sara's family, these individuals unintentionally drew a line of segregation across the room. Edna's face looked as though it would explode. Percy managed to calm her down long enough with a diversion of chilled champagne, while the experienced waiters toted the first course meal, lobster Newberg, piled lavishly on sizzling trays balanced effortlessly above their heads.

"How can they start serving when we haven't even had the reception line; we just arrived?" muttered Sara, knowing that reality's chill had once again enveloped her.

As I looked at her widening, disbelieving steel blue eyes, partially hidden beneath patterned layers of sheer bride's veil, I answered, "They are ready to eat; that's what they want to do, eat, never mind welcoming Doctor and Mrs., the newlyweds; it's human nature, Sara." Then pushing her veil back tenderly, I whispered words of love, remembering that she always expected people to do the proper thing, but usually they didn't, and this was no exception. But our table, the head table, certainly lived up to its expectations! White and pink carnations were intermingled with shades of lavender lilies and pinkish-white roses that were laced with baby's breath. The spectacular arrangements languished and covered the entire front area of the table. Once Sara spied the delightful, detailed arrangements, she forgot the discourteous guests. This was her special time, and no one was going to take away any of its splendor, including her husband's two grown daughters who between glares gasped in disbelief, realizing that their beloved nurturing father had just gotten married, a second time, to a blue-eyed blonde who was somewhat younger in years. Their approval, or lack of it, didn't much matter to Sara now because he was beside her, and that was all that she had wanted since he had first said "Hello," or maybe the second or third time.

Before I knew it, we were being toasted continuously while politely trying to get pieces of buttery iced wedding cake into each other's mouths. Cameras clicked, recording the event as family photos were taken. Now everyone wanted to acknowledge us, since they had been fed, and clamored to get in the pictures. Pausing only once or twice, the string quartet sang its melodic melodies long after midnight with Sara's bobbing head marking the late hour. Guests finally departed, and so did we. With tin cans rattling on the fenders of the car, we managed to find our way to our new home. Actually, I had been living in it for three months prior, wanting to iron out any kinks that insisted on showing up, but there were none. All the while, Sara's face was affixed to her bride's bouquet, which was stuffed with intoxicating gardenias that initiated my sneezing attack. Somewhere in the back of my mind that fragrance, that pungent odor triggered memories of tilling in my mother's garden in the early hours of dawn. Inhaling that annoying odor, I could still see the same little white flowers begging for moistened dirt as the sun rose, and with hoe in hand, I de-weeded and watered until well after dawn. This early morning flower-care was a consequence of coming in at 4:00 in the morning with my buddies. Needless to say, gardening is not a favorite pastime of mine.

Suddenly I forgot the gardenias when Sara blurted out, "Well, I guess that I will be going now; it is getting late." I just stared at her in shock, in amazement, and in horror. I didn't know quite what to say, so I just said anything that came to mind, thinking that maybe she was trying to be funny, but she wasn't.

"Where is it that you are going?" I asked, trying to remain calm yet almost too tired to believe my ears.

"I don't feel that I should stay; I just need to leave," she answered, looking very serious and alarmed. I knew that change was hard for Sara, but I wasn't expecting this, not now, not tonight of all nights!

"Why don't you just take it easy and relax, and if by morning you still feel the same way, then you can leave, and I guess I will go on our honeymoon by myself," I heard myself say. The plane to Puerto Vallarta was scheduled to leave at six-thirty in the morning, only a few hours from now. Had she forgotten all about the trip, about us? Why would she feel this way? I frowned, feeling as though I had just been snatched out of a deep, wonderful romantic dream. Knowing calmness was the answer, I convinced myself that whatever was happening could be resolved. But it had to be figured out first by Sara. Persuading her to do anything against her will was pointless.

"So, if I decide to leave that's all right with you?" she implored, realizing that the choice whether or not to stay was still up to her. She chose sleep instead with all of its intoxication. I slowly breathed a heavy sigh of relief when I felt her head sink effortlessly into the pillow next to me. Since then I have come to the conclusion that maybe, just maybe, she voices her inner feelings in outlandish statements so that I will react, and that this somehow helps her to see just how much I really care. I am so glad that we survived that shaky, first night of our union, and ... Suddenly I felt Sara squeezing my hand and heard the words, "let no man put asunder."

"Polo, isn't she stunning? Do you remember when?" Sara asked me, eyes brimming with silent tears, not needing to finish her sentence.

"That is all that I have been thinking about since I first glanced at Almita," I replied, wondering if Sara knew just how stunning we were together even though I never told her, wondering if any part of the man she married was still visible.

TEACHER CORPS

"Could that be you, Polo, underneath that grayish beard? What happened to your pretty face?" asked Rueben, shocked at the Polo who now stood beside him toting his new wife, Sara, who was strikingly noticeable. With her pale face and blonde hair billowing in the frigid air-conditioning, she had the unique privilege of being jam-packed in a San Antonio hoteliers' convention hall with a diverse group of educators, mostly Mexican-American and African-Americans who hadn't seen each other in thirty some-odd years. It was the reunion of the Teacher Corps, an organization that I belonged to decades ago, centuries ago it seemed, and this was just one of those opportunities that you couldn't let slip away. Needless to say, the twenty-odd phone calls from the reunion committee, as well as the request for recent pictures helped me to decide that this was something that I needed to do. Besides, it was always good to get away from oneself even for just a few days, and so here we were with my buddy Rueben by my side.

"Sara, I would like you to meet Rueben, the current San Antonio Superintendent of Schools, who thirty years ago insisted that he and I leave the confining comfort of the Rio Grande Valley and submit applications to join Teacher Corps, a newly-funded program in San Antonio that was recruiting young people who were qualified and wanted to make a difference."

"Great to meet you," Sara said automatically, reaching for his outstretched hand yet appearing a bit unnerved by his title and introduction. Being a terminal teacher, she was more than aware of what it took to become a superintendent—the ability to balance ever-changing politics by befriending the tokens of power, the temperamental board members.

Rueben, grinning ear to ear, recalled his cleverness. "Remember when I got you to the phone as you were teaching your biology class?

"Yes, how could I forget it?"

"Polo, you have just got to say yes to this ... There is this program; it's federally funded, and they are searching for qualified individuals to reach troubled kids, to motivate them to stay in school. Doesn't that sound like us, you and me? What do you think?" Rueben asked insistently.

What did I think? I couldn't believe my ears; first and foremost, we were not particularly qualified, and second, we were minorities, Mexican-American. Oddly enough, that discrimination factor proved to be our greatest asset. We were selected because of it.

"That was a defining moment for me ..." I hesitated slightly. "And Rueben, if you hadn't wanted something that was impossible, we would have missed all of this." I motioned to other alumni members. Outwardly many had changed like me. But time couldn't touch our inner spirit.

"Polo, that has to be you peering from under that beard, isn't it?" asked a cantankerous, grinning, crystal-eyed lawyer. Molly McBee not only took Teacher Corps by storm but then proceeded to tackle the courts of Texas. Just by looking at her, I knew that she still had every bit of it: the poise, the precision, the fight to make it happen.

"Molly, I didn't think that you would be able to make it with your heavy trial schedule," I said, delighted to see her. Her determination and defiance had set her apart from the pack, making her who she now was instead of almost defeating her as it had in Teacher Corps. Today her attitude was well camouflaged in designer clothes. Her eyes sparkled with risk-taking.

"Sara, this is Molly, the one and only."

Yet Molly couldn't wait.

"Polo, she's so ... But what did you do, when did you?" She then came to a halt, realizing that I must have gotten re-married because she sure didn't look or act like the other one, a bit too young, way too quiet. Trying to be less abrasive, she quietly stated, "Hope you can handle him, Sara. We couldn't." She winked at me, getting her rhythm back.

Sara found herself in awe as she often did when meeting someone who opted to struggle, embracing challenges, even though it wasn't necessary or expected of them because they had been raised in the lap of luxury. You couldn't help but be drawn toward a person like Molly, who was so self-assured, so unassuming, and so friendly; so unlike Sara, who was not terribly confident especially when meeting people for the first time. Her seventh graders did challenge her, but it wasn't exactly on par with living in a jungle or deliberating in front of juries. Grabbing Polo's hand, she was thankful that he was on par with Molly, being a well-respected college professor who was dearly loved by his students. Meeting individuals like Molly was beneficial, because it motivated Sara to push harder.

Conversation eventually gave way to functions, and before I knew it, Sara and I were being ushered to an elegant dinner table complete with our own personal nametags. Alumni encircled us. A generous hand helped me as I sat down, and a pair of warm brown eyes met mine. It was Jollie, my African-American buddy who thirty years ago never left my side.

"Jollie, whatever have you been up to, well, say, the last twenty years?" I asked her, wanting only to hear her soulful thoughts.

"For starters, I just retired. I ... It's my mother," she replied, lowering her eyes. "They found an inoperable lump months ago. But talk about timing ... Just after my mother's diagnosis, the powers that be decided that my lifelong quest of adding that resounding title of principal to my name would became a reality. Yet, once I had it, I didn't want it; all my push was re-directed toward my mother, fighting for her."

"Jollie, I had no idea. I am so sorry to hear about your mother, I ... didn't know," I said, stopping, knowing all too well how hard it is to see a mother slowly fade with cancer, since it had happened to mine.

Before long the loud speaker perched on top of the podium at the head table silenced us, and the recognition ceremony began. Sara's eyes were darting here and there, absorbing everything like a brand new sponge never before seeing so many multi-cultural professionals, so intense. Listening to all of their past and current accomplishments, Sara couldn't help but feel overpowered by what they had done and contributed. "Change Agent" was the catchy phrase that kept wafting from the speakers, signifying not only their role in Teacher Corps, but also embracing the philosophy in their lives. Many in the group had become attorneys, doctors, administrators, and successful business owners all because they wanted to make a difference by opening the minds of other minorities, encouraging them, helping them escape the tightly-fitted jaws of poverty.

Sara couldn't understand why I never talked about this part of my life; it all sounded so exciting compared to her brief college stint at an isolated, all-girls school in Portland, Maine. There she found herself submerged in nursing classes, even though she panicked at the sight of blood and needles and fainted when assisting with any type of operation. Trying to carry on her female, generational family tradition of nursing, she enrolled for two tedious years, taking one involved class after another. The only thing Sara looked forward to were the starch-laden lunches at the hospital, which caused her to fall asleep, irritating the hospital supervisor to no end. Besides gaining weight, the only other diversion was going out at night when the dormitory's den mother nodded off. The would-be nurses then slipped out like slippery noodles, exploring the tiny town in the dead of winter for any trace of male life suitable for non-medical conversation. After two years Sara realized that the neatly-starched, white-pinned cap was not for her, which unnerved her grandmother, aunts, mother, and sister, who all donned the stiff white cap. But Polo's passion was so far-reaching, so timeless; how she longed for him to share just parts of it, but he wouldn't, and that hurt her deeply ...

"We would like to give recognition to those in the group," the speaker's voice faded in and out as I listened without surprise at those who had become distinguished and notable in their individual, chosen fields. There was Vincente who thirty-five years ago had adamantly protested against the Vietnam War but now was an inspiring federal prosecutor. Felippe, who used to challenge his college professors on almost any issue, now headed up University of Colorado where people challenged him, since he was reigning chancellor. And the list went on and on ... For that matter, no one seemed at all surprised with me either when they found out that I had continued in education and obtained my doctorate. It was expected. It shouldn't be; it had drained every bit of my soul, leaving me with almost nothing to give. I wondered if Sara knew.

THE NEEDLE MAN

I f someone had told me three days ago that I would be in this delicate room, I would have denied it. The two carved mahogany chairs were covered with hand-sown tapestry, and next to them stood antique lacquered lamps draped in lace that barely shone. Across the room a velvet green sofa with sinkable cushions begged to be sat upon. The pink-pastel walls hid silver-potted palms in each corner. If I didn't know better, I could easily envision a gorgeous creature slinking in through the doorway other than, of course, my wife, who was fidgeting in one of the high-back chairs, holding her neck and pointing to her back. I guess the chairs were only to look at. My vision quickly vanished when a tall, good-looking younger man walked in and introduced himself as Doctor Gonzalez.

"Have you ever had this procedure done before, Dr. Saenz?" he asked confidently while casting a quick glance at Sara, wondering if she needed treatment as well.

"To be quite frank with you, Doctor, it was my wife's idea to come. I am not sure what to expect, but I need help with my pain, my phantom pain," I said. "Lately it has been unbearable. I just can't seem to function." I redirected my eyes toward the door, not at all sure whether I could handle what was next.

Somewhat relieved that I was still in the room, Sara watched, fearing I might bolt like a wild colt when spoken to for the very first time. Thank

132

goodness she was stubborn like her mother, who was relentless in trying to find an answer to my stump pain. Two days ago while bidding fifty cents during her weekly four-hour bridge marathon, her mother had questioned her card buddies how they battled their persistent pain, not from non-stop card playing but from weathered backs and aching knees. Dr. Gonzalez seemed to be the cure-all, regardless of the fact that his acupuncture practice was in Matamoras, a well-known tequila town just across the border in Mexico. So we took a chance on Dr. Gonzalez, and here we were. From our sofa to the office's sofa took forty minutes, not including the time it took to stop twice for directions to locate the doctor's office. What is it about directions when two different people can give you the exact opposite instructions on how to get to the exact same place? Nonetheless, now her expectations rose like a morning fog on a damp, cold day as she willed this to be the cure that I so desperately needed.

It wasn't a very soothing sight, I must admit, when the crinkling packets of sterile needles were opened and laid beside me on the table, but Dr. Gonzalez's comforting demeanor made me momentarily forget about the tools of his trade.

"I am going to start inserting needles into your waist area first," stated Dr. Gonzalez as I watched drowsily, listening to piped-in Mozart and concentrating on Sara's antics. Being stretched out on a cot-like table had its advantages––you really couldn't see anything as the needles were poked in. But Sara's face told me that the procedure was very intense. Since my prosthesis was off, there was more surface area for the good doctor to jab, and jab, and jab. When he advanced toward my stump, I cringed in pain as the severed nerve endings destroyed my mind-over-matter theory. Gagging, Sara quietly rushed out of the room. She hated needles, and watching me transform into an exploding pincushion was just too much for her.

Not missing a beat, the experienced voice tried to put me at ease, reassuring me that he had done this before, many times. I hoped he had.

"Yes, I was trained in France about ten years ago because there was not an accredited acupuncturist program here in Mexico," said Doctor Gonzalez. "After I finished traditional medical school, I realized that being a plastic surgeon wasn't what I really wanted to do."

Had I heard him right? He chose needles over a scalpel and with so much time to charge unearthly fees? Although I hadn't seen my bill yet, I figured I should probably wait before I lauded him too much. But how did he stay so trim, so dapper, with his work schedule? His white enchanting smile surrounded by a healthy crease-free face could woo a woman in labor––well, maybe one with a broken arm. I was jealous and wanted what he had. As I peered closer, his thick tousled tufts of brown, highlighted hair swept this way and that when the air conditioner blasted it. Everything about the doctor screamed of naturalness. Halting my inspection, the professed forty-year-old going on twenty-five continued.

"I realized there was a big difference between making people beautiful and making people free from pain. So I chose healing over sculpting and have never regretted it."

Merit, simple merit, almost unheard of today, I mulled over in my porcupine stupor. I must have fallen fast asleep because the dream that I had was surreal. I was running and had two healthy legs that worked. It was some kind of race, and I was out in front, then I tripped and fell hard, waking up in a cold sweat. Forgetting where I was, I couldn't figure out why all these silver sewing needles were sticking out of my body in mosaic patterns as Sara peeked through the doorway, reminding me softly where I was.

"You were supposed to rest; the needles stay in for forty minutes," said Sara, trying to camouflage her fear: needles terrorized her, and she was looking at about a hundred or more.

"I'm not feeling any pain right now," I mumbled, being thankful yet fearful, not wanting to get up, knowing the pain would be waiting for me. A buzzer sounded, and a whistling hum could be heard from down the hall. In strolled Dr. Gonzalez with all of his innate happiness. I couldn't stand it any longer.

"Doc, where do you get it? Your outlook, I mean. You just seem so ..." There was no need to finish.

"Oh, I give myself acupuncture. It also keeps you young and heals multi-symptoms throughout the body," answered the doctor.

Sara squirmed, feeling sure that he was a runner, that life-force, that something, a member of the cult. She was addicted as well, wishing that some of her energy would motivate Polo. It did. He ate more.

"Exercise and allowing time for my family also give balance to my heavy workload," continued the doctor. "Oh, yes, and my wife's ever-changing criteria for our half-constructed stucco-built Spanish-style home definitely keeps me on my toes," said the doctor, smiling, wondering if Sara were equally as demanding. Studying the drained, legless professor and his hyper wife who more than made up for his lack of energy, the curious doctor wondered what had trampled him and why he had given up. Pausing, he then carefully extracted the numerous needles from the swollen pressure point areas on the still one-legged form in front of him.

After the last needles had been artfully removed from both sides of my temples, Doctor Gonzalez politely exited in his doctor-like fashion. Thanking Mozart for his concert, I gritted my teeth and slowly stood up. My stump didn't hurt. Much to my amazement, it didn't ache; the pain was gone. It was as though my body had been switched with another's; whose, I wondered? Sara held her breath and then clung to me as though I were the last life preserver on a sinking ship.

I whispered triumphantly, "I am not hurting," hoping that this might be the antidote I had been searching for: slender, silver, jabbing needles. After convincing Sara to loosen her grip, I thought she looked more like the patient. Attaching my prosthesis, I waited for the squeezing pain, but it didn't happen. Untying my thin white gurney, I watched my goose bumps fade as I donned my comfortable jeans, not realizing how pleasant it was to be fully clothed once again. As Sara looked into my eyes, I felt happiness and sadness knowing how much I had robbed from her; she hadn't deserved or bargained on this draining partner in our relationship ... pain. Maybe now there was a way. Maybe our life could change, sharing love and laughter instead of regret and tears.

Doctor Gonzalez suddenly reappeared and instructed his assistant to usher us toward the virtuous payment window. On the way I spied the needles in their discarded bin, reassured that they hadn't been used before me and weren't going to be used after me. Halfway down the corridor, Sara couldn't take her eyes off the posters with the flawless botox girls and their advertised creaseless smiles. Then she remembered seeing a documentary where one botoxed victim had continual, splitting migraine headaches after the acclaimed miracle-like procedure. So much for miracles. Beginning to feel those migraine headaches, she finally decided to ignore her own time-etched hieroglyphics and let the markings remain unaltered. Pleased that she had made a decision, she turned toward me, giving me one of those "did you remember?" nudges, and I hadn't. Hearing the good doctor's spirited laugh as it resonated down the hallway, I signaled to him, and before I knew it, he was by my side. Oh, to have legs like his that worked in unison without fear of falling, I thought, watching him in awe, almost forgetting about it. "It" had been on my chin for months, and when I shaved, it always got nicked, making me look like a twenty-one-year-old with my first intense breakout.

"Sorry, I don't do chins," the busy doctor replied as I pointed to it and recounted its stubborn history. Noting its size and consistency, he said, "But I have this buddy, a dermatologist in the states, who I am sure could minimize it; let my secretary give you his number."

Back at the virtuous payment window, I flashed my trusty insurance card yet only got a stare with a negative shake. A young Mexican head didn't seem to be a bit surprised by my intentions.

"We don't take insurance from the United States," the voice in broken English informed me, so Andrew Jackson showed his face a few times——five to be exact. Feeling uncomfortable because of my ignorance, I motioned to Sara.

"Can you believe it? My insurance isn't any good here."

I handed her the receipt. Her face didn't even flinch.

"Well, Doctor Gonzalez is building a new house, and you have just contributed to his house payment," she said, grinning, thinking about the margaritas down the street. Bothered by her indifference, I wondered what it was about a woman's psyche; nothing disturbs them regarding bills as long as they don't have to pay them. But just then the lights went out; I mean the whole street was darkened, and all the electricity vanished. Now you have to understand my concern; we were right in front of the elevators, just about to get in. If I hadn't been so slow, we would have been inside, trapped four floors up. Mexican electricity isn't backed up by generators, so when it stops you stop. I guess that explains why very few people were using the elevator; most of them scurried toward the winding stairs, which seemed like an excellent idea.

But Sara froze, grabbed my arm, and whispered, "We almost got in, what ... look ... look behind you, outside, do you see it?" she said, her voice quivering. An electrical wire detached itself from a pole and spun wildly in the air, spitting fiery sparks as though it had something to say. With our jaws ajar, we witnessed an amazing unscheduled fireworks display that lasted for ten minutes. Slowly recovering, Sara thanked God for my slow gait, vowing never again to use the elevators in Mexico regardless of how many stairs she might have to climb.

"A margarita sounds really good right now," she proclaimed, thankful to be still breathing as we descended to the street level like two mice in a winding maze trying to find the opening. It was right in front of us. When we got outside, others didn't seem at all disturbed by the brilliant, light show. It probably happens all the time, I thought.

Sounds and smells of peoples' livelihoods filled the air. Everywhere you looked big brown eyes lit up hungry brown faces that tried eagerly to get your attention. Colorful handmade items made from everything imaginable were waved in the air while shouts of "Mister" rang out; desperate voices yelled desperate prices; you had to barter; they expected it. As we meandered down the street, skillful knives were whittling lifelike figurines out of wood, glass-blown pottery was being twisted this way and that, while beautifully-shaped marble was transformed into animal figures right before our eyes. Such creativity, such poverty. Wafts of cooking meat pervaded the air. Skewers of thick, juicy beef kabobs mingled with onions and peppers appeared on makeshift grills that were mounted on wooden slats on loaded-down bicycle handle bars. The bicycle-chef waived his wares in the air, shouting out, "Muy bueno," meaning "very good" in Spanish.

Sara stopped. She was starving.

"Que cuesta?" she asked, knowing a bit of Spanish from bantering with our on-again, off-again maid who showed up when she needed the money.

But before the sale could continue, I mumbled, "No, gracias," since I knew what could happen if Sara's craving overtook her logic.

"Don't you remember when your folks got Montezuma's revenge: their forty-eight hour bathroom tour of duty accompanied with its extreme dehydration?" I asked, wondering how she could forget the gruesome details. "Just because they ate lunch at an open-air market while sight-seeing in Mexico." I recalled her Dad's knowledgeable advice: when in Mexico, don't do as the locals do. Eat only at a bona fide restaurant where there's a better chance that the cooks have washed their hands with soap and cooked the food completely. Sara just tossed her head in defiance, not really listening to Polo's logic because, of course, he was always right. I waited for a look of "Oh yeah, you're right," but there wasn't one. Unfortunately, this is a professional hazard in our profession. Teachers and certainly professors are never wrong––hardly ever. Well, how could they be? All day, every day, they tell students what to do and how to do it, expecting comfortable control with no exceptions. Since we both were innately and professionally educators, listening to each other was not a comfortable option for us.

"Look at these hues of colors," said Sara, having lost her appetite as she watched purples, bright yellows, pinks, and oranges cascading down makeshift walls and separating squished buildings. "Nothing blends together; so unlike the choreographed motifs on the other side of the border," she remarked.

"You always notice the brighter things," I answered, so thankful that she was drawn to the beauty, regardless of where it was. Her artistic side always showed itself. She was so aware, so absorbed with everything; negativity didn't have a chance with her. On the other hand, negativity consumed me like a flame's flicker on dry parched timber. Then out of the corner of my eye, I spied him, which was truly amazing since he had been the topic of our more frivolous conversations for months.

"Well, can you believe it?" I asked, knowing it was destiny––a barber and open for business. The well-groomed, trim figure motioned us toward his shop entrance as his apron ruffled slightly in the wind. Flashing me one of his ear-to-ear grins, he couldn't wait to get me in his swiveling chair. I think barbers get some type of adrenalin rush every time they see rumpled hair that needs trimming, and he was no exception. Usually my older sister, Amberina, who was a whiz at cutting hair, kept me on a grooming schedule; however, lately she hadn't been bothering me. Secretly I think it was her way of keeping her fingers in my life as well as my hair. I guess the interest level had died down a bit. Then before I knew it, Senor Lopez twirled me around in his chair and gently slathered my face with foamy facial cream because the shave came first.

Sara's eyes widened as the skilled barber sharpened his blade back and forth on a serop, a piece of rawhide attached to his chair, like he was getting ready to cut a Thanksgiving turkey. She was so thankful that Senor Lopez had convinced me to lose my hairy face. My gray-scraggly whiskers made me look so worn-out, so bedraggled. I remembered the first time she saw me——so clean-shaven, every hair in place, tucked and trimmed and perfect. Yet time seemed to have turned all that caring into disregard. Although this was a pale glimmer of hope, I was actually getting a haircut. Could the treatment really have brightened my perspective so quickly? Listening to me laugh at Senor Lopez's antics almost made Sara cry. It had been months since she had seen me laugh or cry or react to anything. It was like my frozen face was thawing from a winter's freeze.

"I wondered when you were going to let your chiseled cheekbones show themselves again," said Sara, delighted that Grandpa had vanished and her handsome husband had reappeared.

Senor Lopez's fingers were synchronized to a barber's beat, and tufts of speckled hair came tumbling down. Looking quite pleased with himself, Senor handed me a mirror as I sat in the barber chair. The lines seemed to have faded, my face had a profile, and my old self peeked through. I couldn't believe the difference. Time had numbed my awareness. But Sara noticed, and it showed in her moist eyes. Seeing her watch me so intently made me realize how much she still cared; I wondered why. How could she when I had given up; why shouldn't she? I guess it was her stubbornness, her refusal to give in. I'm grateful for it every day, even though I usually complain about it. Maybe I could make more of an effort and connect with something other than pain now that it was gone. I didn't want to get my hopes up, because too many times, too many well-meaning remedies had lasted only a few days or a few weeks. The pain always returned with a vengeance. Slowly the barber swiveled me around, flashing his silver-capped white teeth, looking like he had won the lottery.

"Mucho major (much better)," he said with a satisfied voice, hoping this Mexican-American would keep it that way for the lady.

As I paid him, he hesitated and gave me a proud look. Mexican men are always proud, if nothing else; I wondered if any of my pride would resurface.

"You have it in your eyes again," commented Sara as she wrapped her fingers around my relaxed hand.

"What, my youth?" I replied.

"Yes, that too." She smiled. "But the glaze is gone. You know, that trance of yours that takes over when you are in combat with yourself."

"Sara," I said softly as I turned my head, capturing her eyes, "I know it hasn't been easy for you lately, well, for quite a while, yet I think there may still be a chance for me, for us, if I can just hold on. Maybe the acupuncture will do it." I wanted to believe that it would. Holding her hand, I could feel her strength flowing through me like a prescribed drug, giving me a natural high.

"You know He's the only way and the only answer," she replied, her compassionate Lord being her constant source of strength, the reason why she could still give to Polo, knowing she wouldn't receive.

"I know," I answered and believed it, although when I hurt, everything was blocked out, including my faith.

"Look, look over there, a papoose on that lady's back," said Sara, thinking it was a bundle of fruit, but then it moved. The lady's bundle seemed content at the moment; little did he know of his dismal fate. She couldn't imagine squatting on the sidewalk, begging for money, while strangers peered at her with jaded curiosity and pity. "How can she do it?"

"These people don't have a choice. Poverty forces the hand. Sometimes both," I said, remembering how hard it was to be poor. "You know, Mama would never let us accept money or food from anyone. Our hands were working, working hard," I said. It was very difficult for me to watch this poor, helpless woman; I felt a sickness deep inside me, knowing that the only thing that separated me from her was pure, random luck. I was born on the side of the border where there was opportunity, quality education, and government handouts. But here ... leaning over, I filled the woman's cup with clinging change. Our eyes met for an instant, which filled me with choking gratitude since the claws of poverty no longer clung to me. Not far from the huddled figure, there were other hands, little hands that reached up as little voices cried, "Mister," hoping that anything would be placed in their palms.

"Sara, these are the desperate eyes and faces that continually haunt me. This was the main reason that I didn't want to come across and get the treatment. Being here has just stirred up my anger against poverty and its injustice——wealthy Mexicans who commonly disregard their own, the have-nots. You are either very well off or very poor; a middle-class doesn't exist here. Once the line is drawn, it is rarely crossed, as though most of the population is invisible."

While listening intently, Sara's gaze fastened onto a whittling carver as he demonstrated his raw talent, turning a simple piece of notched wood into a religious depiction of the Last Supper.

"Polo, but there are trickles of hope. Just look at that handiwork," she said, motioning to the carver's creation. "These simple yet creative people have so much to give regardless of the poverty," she whispered, vowing never again to have her own pity party. She had everything compared to those around her.

"Their devout Catholic faith sustains them, giving them strength regardless of their outer circumstances," I said, recalling how Mama's strong Christian values were probably the only reason why my family had survived at all.

Sara felt like she was in another time zone. Thoughts she had previously gnawed away at her. For a long time now, she had suspicions that many of her disadvantaged students lived like this, even with government subsidies. But she never had witnessed it before; now she couldn't dismiss it. She was in it. She needed to talk about it.

"Polo, these children remind me of my students; they have that same look, that uncertain stare," Sara gushed. "At school the boys, well ... their clothes are neon indicators: baggy pants, way beyond baggy, which probably belonged to their fathers or older brothers. Even when it gets cold, the clothes hardly change, except for maybe two t-shirts instead of one under the very baggy sweatshirts or jackets, if any at all. The little girls, they seem to try harder to disguise their t-shirt wardrobe by streaking their hair with reddish tones and experimenting with heavy make-up. You should see them at the library, gaping at the magazine families with curiosity and guarded disbelief.

"I know. You are describing how my friends and I grew up," I said. "We knew that we were different yet never realized how different until we went to college. There we witnessed the real magazine people, living comfortably, never worrying about food or warmth, only about maintaining minimum grades or eligible females. Those females seemed to be on a compiled list that was taped to their foreheads. My list consisted of girls who looked like they could cook, so I could get fed daily without spending money that I didn't have. I learned quickly what being a have-not from the Valley truly meant.

"You know, that's probably why my kids are always munching on their annoying gum," she said. "They are hungry. I will never forget the time when I asked one of my munching students to come in for tutoring; his reply stunned me. He couldn't because he was being shuffled again. His biological parents were in jail, and he was up for grabs, but his relatives weren't grabbing. His honesty caught me off guard, making me feel ridiculous since I was only concerned about his grades when no one was concerned about him. But as time went on, he proved to be resilient, passed, and went on to high school. Like you said, there are the have-nots who truly have not but somehow survive."

"Not to change the subject, but right now I am a have," I interrupted, having an appetite that needed some authentic Mexican food made in a good, old Mexican kitchen. My ravaged stomach hadn't been fed since our hurried breakfast of toast and java. An enticing aroma had demanded my attention as we approached Arturo's, an infamous Mexican restaurant. We quickly secured a linen-covered table that was attached to a gold-toothed grinning Mexican waiter.

After sipping on a Juervo-Gold tequila-laden margarita complete with stuffed olives and a salt-coated rim, I watched her. Her passion for life was intoxicating: she never missed a single detail. Her eyes widened in pure delight as she smelled sauteed onions on sizzling steaks that passed by. Her fingertips kept the beat of mariachi harmonies as they bounced their bows off their violins, even the bow that was slightly out of tune. Colors, they never escaped her. She couldn't take her eyes off the muted patterns of greens and pinks as they dove-tailed throughout the room. How I envied her since I didn't even know how to peek. Could she teach me? Could I learn? I looked away and watched nothing.

THE BIG C

I was certainly getting attention now, more than I had anticipated. Feeling very uncomfortable, I averted my eyes as Doctor Peel prodded my chin, mumbling under his breath about how it really looked. I had taken Doctor Gonzalez's advice and selected Doctor Peel, who was one of two dermatologists on the university's pre-approved insurance provider list. The first listed doctor wasn't seeing new patients. So, I figured most professors didn't have enough facial breakouts to cause any major concern at the college. However, I was now very concerned as Doctor Peel turned it this way and that. Then scurrying in, Dr. Peel's nurse handed him my statistics.

"Your blood pressure is very high," the doctor noted as he studied my collected data taken by his competent nurse. "Way too high," he said again, hesitating then picking up the phone and dialing. After a brief conversation, a yellow blinking light seemed to flash from his eyes, and he cautioned me, saying, "A complete physical needs to be done before it can be removed; I have set up an appointment for you with Doctor Albright."

With that, he disappeared like a full moon at dawn. So much for the bedside manner, I thought, guessing that my five minutes were up yet never imagining the twists and turns that lay ahead of me. But as chance would have it, Doctor Albright's office was in the very same medical building, so I didn't even have enough time not to go to the just-made, necessary appointment. Feeling no control regarding it, I braced myself for the next round of procedures like a novice boxer waiting for his first unknown competitor. It was ring time before I knew it, as a tidy nurse cordoned me into an examination room packed with a blood pressure machine, stethoscope, assorted vials, and long needles. Meeting my competition, I quickly felt the jabs poking their way into my arms, my buttocks, and any other available vein. It was as though the nurse enjoyed her brief moment of power, making me squirm. After all, I had interrupted a tense, doctor-nurse moment when I arrived. Of course, it had to happen just before my physical. Take a deep breath, I told myself. Welcome to your fight.

"You are going to be tested for diabetes," Ms. Tidy said, I guess because I was a bit overweight, forty bits to be exact. "In addition, your glucose sugar level will be examined, as well as your blood platelets, which help determine blood clotting. Your spleen and liver will also be tested to check how." She was gushing medical jargon like a newly-opened bottle of champagne. I just wanted to stuff the cork back in. Tiring quickly, my ears weren't hearing, and I just wanted her to do what she needed to do, not to discuss it, but her matter-of-fact tone rattled on like a worn-out tape.

"Being over fifty, your PSA [prostate specific antigen] level needs to be determined before we can proceed," I heard the tape say. "You need to go see a urologist of your choice and have a complete battery of tests done before we can continue with it."

All of this because of a stubborn growth on my chin that refused to heal. The enraged sore just needed to be removed instead of treating it like a contagious malignancy. Now I knew how a leper felt. I should start looking for the colony, I thought. Would the tape know of its whereabouts? No, the tape only spewed out information in staccato, reminding me of Sara's piano playing––her Bach with its short, quick notes of exactness. Once the tape stopped, I quickly exited, just wanting to get home where there would be no more instructions, only questions. I wasn't disappointed.

"Oh, let me see your beautiful chin," Sara piped as soon as she heard my return-home noises. "But why is it still there? You have been gone all afternoon," she yelped like a little puppy, feeling very frustrated, wondering where I had been.

"It's very complicated," I answered, just wanting to change the subject yet knowing that wouldn't happen until every annoying detail had been told. With Sara's urging, rather insistence, the college's list of insurance providers was once again staring me down, but this time it was the urologists. After scouring the list, the PSA man of choice happened to be in Brownsville, almost right next to the college. My being inconvenienced was not going to be a legitimate out. Later that evening, when I was just fading away from urologist mania, Percy, my father-in-law, who usually clarified my thoughts, called, so I listened.

"The PSA, yeah, I just had mine taken, and it was a bit high," said Percy "My doctor gave me some medication, and it has since gone down, but I get it checked every three months. You know, Polo, it is an indicator of the big *C*." The nurse hadn't revealed that intricate connection. Percy's words reverberated in my ears, deafening me, all intentions of not going suddenly vanished. I set up an appointment the next day.

But those three letters now possessed me, and I would never be the same. Sara did her best to calm me, but her well-meaning words were like the smell of sizzling hamburger to a starving child; it just wasn't enough–– my panic was full blown.

"Once you have been to the urologist, all of your exams will be finished," Sara said, putting on her confident face. "Then you can return to Doctor Peel and get the growth removed once and for all," her mouth whispered, thinking I was listening, but I wasn't. Her attempted wit, the "exam" word, didn't even get a rise out of me, which was unusual since I was usually making or grading exams. Instead my mind raced ahead, turning this way and that, looking for exits, but there were none, and I knew it.

"It's genetic, the cancer, my mother," I blurted out. The memories welled up inside me like an untamed river. "It was all so unexpected. No one knew what was wrong with her, and she just didn't get well. Test after test revealed nothing, so we all just thought she was tired, tired of trying, tired of fighting, tired of life. Her energy vanished as if by choice. Initially I thought it was her way of getting my attention, and she got it. It was the way she ..." Mama's words weighed down my thoughts while she closed in on me.

"Polo, I made your favorite bread pudding with plenty of raisins and cinnamon, the way you like it," Mama said as I listened to the urgency in her voice. "Your new classes, your students, I haven't heard about..." Then she paused as I took a quick breath.

"Mama," I heard myself say, "I will be there today, right after my last class, which ends at seven." It felt like my cruise control switch had just been activated. "Only you know how to make bread pudding exactly right," I said, smelling the warmed cinnamon as it wrapped itself around the raisins.

"I was exhausted, but it didn't matter. Everything stopped, because I knew she needed me," I said out loud. "So, lecture or not, I saved my best for Mama since her day started once our eyes met. It seemed the sixty-minute drive to McAllen got shorter and shorter; often I was lucky to have made it at all."

My devotion for my mama was driven by a soul-connecting love that refused to be replaced, even with death. Sara knew this. She watched my inner torment for twelve years, but Mama somehow stubbornly remained between us like a grown, live-in child who refused to leave. But I had no idea that Mama had somehow also contributed to my life-threatening driving style. Now, I knew why all of her nagging about speed never changed anything. I couldn't change.

"So that's why you drive the way that you do," Sara said, realizing that speed represented valuable time to me, fleeting time with Mama. The safety car-length issue would not be discussed again. Instead she promised herself that she would always drive.

"The distance was insignificant. I could manage it," I said. "Then Mama refused to eat. It was as though she was testing me because I had always been the appointed one in our family to fix things whether complicated or unjust. But this was different; it defied Mama's core: her love of eating and preparing food. With food she demonstrated how much she loved us and how far she could stretch what little we had. Her homemade beans and tortillas were a valuable commodity, attracting familiar noises in our neighborhood. You know, Sara, if your cooking were any indicator, you would never know that you even liked me."

Sara grimaced. She hated to cook and never did. It was just so boring. Oh, more minus points, she thought, knowing that she didn't even come close to Mama's cooking prowess even with a stuffed refrigerator full of possibilities.

"Well, you know how claustrophobic I get in the kitchen," replied Sara. "Hovering in a limited space while deciphering exact recipes over a heated stove isn't for me. Cooking takes time and adds weight; it is not a love gauge. But you know my dislike for cooking is genetic. My mother hates to cook as well, yet her love..." she gushed as she recited her mother's most endearing quote, which had been passed down from her great-grandmother. "I love you up to the sky and down again."

Often Sara would wrap her confident arms around my fallen shoulders, whispering the love code into my needy ears. On rare occasions after a heated disagreement, I would whisper the code back, reassuring her that I still loved her.

Again I thought I heard Mama's persistent voice, "Broiled codfish with lemon sauce, and maybe some chicken soup, with vegetables. But I am really not hungry; you shouldn't go to all that trouble, Polo." Sometimes the heart says what the mind can't, and this was one of those times.

"That is why I had to be with her every day, just to make sure that she would eat," I said, wanting Sara to understand Mama's declining condition. "Luby's and I became steadfast buddies. After a while I automatically ordered food for both of us, and the attractive cashiers always joked about my mysterious eating partner, wanting to meet her. They couldn't have imagined who was waiting for her food and how much it mattered. Then one exhausting day after stubbornly following the daily racetrack up to McAllen, I panicked. After knocking on Mama's door, I patiently waited, yet nothing happened. I checked to make sure that I had the right door, the right house ... I did. Then the bothered door just glared at me, asking, Does it look like anyone is here? Its rudeness stunned me, yanking me out my exhaustion. As I turned around, a concerned or nosy neighbor yelled from their watchful window that Papa had just taken Mama to the hospital. Everything just went blank. Somehow I managed to make my way through the maze-like corridors of the manicured hospital, although I almost got run over by a scurrying doctor who had just examined Mama.

"'She just collapsed, and numerous tests have been done, but as of yet they have revealed nothing,' said the scowling doctor, who rightly assumed that I was the appointed one.

"Sara, she was in a coma-like state, and Papa, Papa's face was coated with terror and loss; he didn't know what to do. So, I had to know. Feeling invisible without Mama, Papa needed me; I had never felt that need before. Burying him with hugs and soft assurances, I felt his soul collapse. Calming Papa down was the only thing that mattered. After his sobbing stopped, I began to ask pertinent questions, expecting answers. There were none. The doctors really couldn't figure it out. So the two of us waited, talked, and waited, yet nothing changed. Mama was in a coma, hooked up to a life-support system, and no one could tell me why. As hours crawled by, finally, a white, crisp, well-ironed jacket-clad doctor entered the room like hot air from a covered pot rising quickly, eager to get away. His elitist attitude annoyed me to no end, and it is probably why I still dislike doctors to this day.

"'You need to make a decision,' said the doctor, assuming that I was an ignorant, uneducated Mexican. Little did he know that I packed a Ph.D.

"'What are you trying to say?' I asked, trying hard not to explode in his face.

"'Well, your options are limited since you have no health insurance, and we don't know what is wrong with her,' said the uncomfortable doctor as I glared at him.

"That did it. He ignited my fuse. 'Why do you assume that we have no health insurance?' I asked. 'Do you know that you are talking to an educated professional? Ph.D.?' For once I used my title. It rose in my mouth, and I spit it out. Suddenly the embarrassed doctor softened his tone.

"'Well, I just thought ... I mean, you know, most––'

"I interrupted him, 'No, I don't know. Why, because my father can't keep up with your dialogue? Well, I can, and yes we do have options,' I said angrily. Then the doctor's air pocket abruptly lowered, knowing that I completely understood him: he had nothing to say."

"So were you politely escorted out of the hospital?" asked Sara, knowing how my rage could devour me. "And Mama, what happened? I mean, what did you decide to do?"

"To be honest, I didn't know what to do because what the doctor had said was true enough. Papa didn't have extensive health insurance, although that just made me want to fight harder. Mama was my whole life. Without her it didn't matter. So, during the next three hours, I questioned and re-questioned. Then it came to me; I knew what to do. Meanwhile

Papa had collapsed next to Mama, holding her weakened hand as though for the first time and the last. As I watched the two entwined figures, everything stopped; the three of us seemed to be clinging to a mental shipwreck. But a speck of land was visible; it would be Mama who decided if and when her life ended. She had always been in control and still was at her post. So kneeling down beside her on her unoccupied side, I began the only conversation that now mattered.

"'Mama, you are in the hospital, lying here in a coma, and the doctors don't know what is wrong with you. Papa and I are here, and the doctors have put you on life support. Your condition, it's critical, Mama. I know that Papa has done his best to provide for all of us, usually working three jobs instead of one. Yet what he needs, he doesn't have, which is extensive health insurance in order to keep you attached to the life support system.' While creeping tears clogged my nose and mouth, I agonized, knowing that I had to continue. 'Mama, they want me to decide when to remove the plug that is keeping you alive, but I won't do it. Papa can't, and there is no one else. Mama, that leaves only you; you must decide what you want to do. If you can't wake up, I will understand, go freely and peacefully, knowing that I will always take care of Papa and the girls. You have my word. Mama, if there is any way that you can wake up, now would be an excellent time to do it.'

"There, it was done. My heart had finished. Then leaning over, I softly kissed Mama, sensing it would be for the last time. Slowly I also kissed Papa's cheek, knowing he wouldn't wake up until he had to. Neither the doctor nor the nurse ever returned, so I hoped that Papa would not be disturbed. Numb, I headed for Papa's house. Tonight I would awaken the rude door, not caring what it had to say."

"But why did you leave?" asked Sara, knowing she would have stayed.

"It was just too much, too much sadness, too much pain, too much love," I said, sensing her surprise. "But no one could have imagined what happened the next day. My horrible nightmare flipped into a fantasy. Not wanting to face my worst fears, I forced myself to return to the hospital. The long corridor to Mama's room seemed even chillier than the night before. As I got closer, suddenly the elitist doctor bustled over to me with eyes as wide as an owl, telling me that Mama had woken up. My ears were sure that they had misunderstood, but my sudden adrenalin rush assured me that they hadn't. It was true. Reaching Mama's room, I immediately fell into two waiting pairs of shaking arms. She looked at me and spoke. Her voice hadn't changed a bit. It knew it was back in control.

"'Polo, your father told me that you would be arriving shortly. I've been anxious to tell you both about this dream; I had it last night ...' She paused. 'I kept hearing a voice encouraging me to wake up, and then I guess I did because I wanted to know who was talking to me. Papa was fast asleep, and the only things that I saw were tubes swinging this way and that. I starting calling out and a nurse ran in who looked like she was hallucinating. I guess I scared her. Polo, do you know anything about this dream?' she asked, but when her eyes locked onto mine, she knew. I was her dream. Papa looked dazed and drained, as he kept studying Mama, wondering if she were indeed his beloved Marcella who came back from the other side. He just wanted things to be as they were; he wanted to take his beloved wife home, where she belonged, erasing the last twenty-four hours forever from his consciousness. Getting his wish within hours, Papa witnessed the elitist doctor signing Marcella's release papers. The unnerved doctor hesitated slightly, giving Papa a puzzled look, wanting some of Papa's magic.

"After the coma scare, everyone thought that Mama would improve because the ailment that had almost beaten her had seemingly vanished. However, our hopes tumbled when it reappeared, infecting healthy body parts that previously had been spared. First her heartbeat became irregular as her kidneys malfunctioned. Then her lungs weren't expanding, making it difficult for her to breathe regularly. It was just one thing after another. Every week a different system collapsed, exasperating doctors, nurses, and the eight of us. My daily routine often included visits to the hospital on the days that the stoic door on Papa's house remained silent. It finally quit talking to me after I physically abused it, kicking it hundreds of times. But one day when the door did open, I saw Mama sitting in the chair. Then all my hope emptied."

"Do you mean the chair with wheels?" asked Sara, saddened, remembering her own grandmother, who also ended up in the chair. But not because she had given up. Her stubborn spirit had never heard those words. Yet her frail body had and just couldn't hold her up any longer. "Remember Grammy, how she sat, curled in her chair, her permanent partner? Although her mind was far from curled, it was sharp, witty, and notorious for its impromptu current event quizzes. Grammy knew the details about the details. If you didn't have an opinion on a particular issue, you would soon develop one. I will never forget when you first met Grammy. Not only did she want to know your political and personal views but your intentions as well. Your reaction should have been framed. Watching, I considered rescuing you, but after about fifteen minutes, you and Grammy could have teamed up to anchor the nightly news. Her tender smile and welled-up eyes told me that you were a keeper, the one. With men, Grammy was like a Geiger counter, detecting golden hearts or ones with just a few fine veins of silver. Oh, I didn't mean to go on about Grammy; it was just when you mentioned the chair ..."

"Even though time allowed me only one visit with your grandmother, I felt drawn to her, her stubbornness and her refusal to give up," I replied. "Sara, more than anything else, I also wanted Mama to have meaning in her life. But when she didn't even try, I was destroyed. Mama didn't need her wheelchair like Grammy; her legs worked just fine; it was her spirit ...

"A home plan was conceived. Samuel, my older brother, was the only one out of seven who wasn't working or redirecting adolescents at the time. He was duly elected to fill the position of daily caregiver, a paid position, which turned out to be beneficial for both. Samuel needed the money, and Mama needed the help during the day. At night Papa's love took over. To bathe Mama he somehow figured out a way to hoist her up on an apparatus much like the way he hoisted cars out of ditches. Who would have thought that his part-time tow-truck operator skills would come in handy off the road? Each one of us tried to reach Mama with love, laughter, and hope, but it just wasn't enough. Never knowing what to expect, uncertainty and I stared each other in the face every day until that one night. Mama had just finished some mashed potatoes and meatloaf that I encouraged her to eat, feeding her. Afterwards we talked, but all I could hear were her eyes, which told me to prepare for an ending. Sensing that it was my last time to hold her, I couldn't bear it––instinctively turning my face away. I didn't want her to see my paralyzing fear.

"At that moment Mama guided my frightened hand toward her weary heart, asking, 'Promise me that you will take care of Papa, the girls, and your brothers for me?'

"Praying that something would come out, I waited, but nothing did. Her words just ripped through my mind like a tornado on a desert's surface. Here was this woman who had inspired, shaped, and cherished me for fifty-five years and now wanted me to promise. Anger welled up inside me. My mind snapped. My love ached, since it all belonged to her. Mama's hand started tightening its loving grip, so I forced myself to look at her.

"'I promise.' What else could I do? She demanded an answer."

Sara looked as if she were listening to a daytime soap opera, so many expressions flooding every facet of her face. Although there was no time for a commercial break, I hadn't made the critical connection yet.

"Well, the drawn-out hours of that night crept by as Papa finished his hoisting bathing ritual. Mama's spirit became weaker and weaker as mine became mightier. I vowed never to leave her. Samuel, who had never offered to spend the night, must have sensed a change as well because he stayed with me. While Mama slept I was vigilant, checking, always checking, making sure that she breathed and had a pulse. Exhausted, my body craved sleep, but my mind rejected it. After many hours that seemed like years, Samuel somehow persuaded me to leave my vigil because of a full schedule of classes that awaited me in the morning. Assuring me that he would perform the night watchman's duties, Samuel took over. Before leaving, I tenderly kissed Mama on the lips, taking a mental, camera-like picture of every delicate feature on her drained face. Kissing Mama on the mouth came naturally to me ever since I was a young boy regardless of the ridicule it caused me. My friends thought it very unnatural and odd. I couldn't imagine kissing my mama any other way. Papa didn't seem to mind, so why should anyone else? With its worn tires, my ten-year-old Lumina led the way home. I merely followed. After about thirty minutes, I suddenly felt my chest tighten, my stomach lurch, and my mind stop. My hands momentarily left the steering wheel, and I skidded off the shoulder, landing in a bunch of gangly bushes. Startled but certain there was someone sitting right beside me, I turned; it was Mama. Sprays of lavender, her favorite after-bath lotion, permeated the air while her soft fingers touched my quivering cheeks. Not comprehending what was happening didn't matter to me. I didn't care. I just didn't want it to end.

"Softly Mama's voice said, 'Polo, you know how much I love you, but I had to tell you while gazing into your knowing eyes. I was given extended time.' As her form started fading, I heard the words, 'Your promise, remember your promise.' There was nothing then but cold, slicing silence. Begging her not to leave me, I reached for her, grabbing handfuls of sweetened air. Her sweet smell evaporated. She was gone. The ending had come without anyone's permission. Sobbing uncontrollably, I now knew that I was utterly alone, abandoned. My joy, laughter, and purpose had evaporated also with Mama's lavender scent, leaving behind should have's and what if's. The worn-out tires now knew that they were really on their own since my eyes were swelling wells of emotion. With God's guidance I somehow made it home and was greeted by the incessant ringing of the phone. Reluctantly I answered it.

"It was Samuel.

"'Mama——'

"'Samuel, I know. Mama is gone.'

"'But how did you know?' cried Samuel. 'It just happened about thirty minutes ago.'

"'Mama came to me. I felt her. Papa, what about Papa?' I asked, wanting to turn right back around, wishing I had never abandoned my post.

"'He doesn't know; it all happened so fast. I just didn't know what to do,' said Samuel. 'What should I do?'

"'Don't wake him; he will fall apart. I will be there in the morning to take care of everything. Can you do it? Can you hang on until I get there?' I asked, listening to Samuel's voice heaving and shaking like relentless waves pounding a shoreline.

"'I don't want to do this,' Samuel blurted out. 'It should be you; you should have been the one to cradle Mama in your arms as she gave up. You are the one who could handle this. You would know what to do and say. I——'

"'Samuel, I will be there as soon as I can,' I said as Samuel mumbled something incoherently.

"My mind said go to Samuel, but my body didn't listen; it couldn't. So I slept for a few hours and then mentally prepared myself for chaos. I wasn't disappointed. By the time I arrived the next morning, everyone was there. It seemed Mama had done quite a bit of visiting before she finally left. All of my sisters, Amberina, Avera, Tina, and Aylvia, felt her near them, and

Tito was woken out of a deep dream-filled sleep with Mama's goodbyes. My brothers acted like they were hypnotized, staring straight ahead at nothing. My sisters cried and hugged, maybe out of desperation or guilt, I didn't know. They all had families and kids, so time had been a sensitive issue for them. Now they had to live with their choices, and I embraced mine. For the last five years, Mama always came first, and she knew it. The only choice that I regretted was leaving Mama in her final hours, although I kept my promise to Mama and remained strong for everyone, never finding the time to weep or say my own goodbyes. All seven needed my support, especially Papa. My aching love for Mama would have to remain hidden like a guarded secret surrounded by sentries."

Sara remained still, knowing how much I still agonized over losing my beloved Mama. My drenching love for her consumed me even though it had been eight years since her death. Never experiencing a traumatic loss of her own, Sara had never known its ripping emptiness. Yet if her mother were to die, she hoped that she wouldn't deny love or forget how to give love. My longing had turned to bitterness coated with untamed anger. I couldn't reach outstretched arms; I couldn't see them. Each day, Sara's sadness widened, aching for the love that she had lost, realizing that it had never been hers.

Needing to finish, I forced it out. It was choking me like an undetected, swallowed fish bone. The *C* word.

"After Mama's death there were still so many unanswered questions, and I needed answers. The doctors were extremely reluctant, but that only made me more determined. Finally, I was debriefed by the harassed doctor.

"'Your mother's symptoms can be detected in a particular type of cancer; one that is irreversible, ravaging the body, sapping every morsel of strength out of it. This is the closest diagnosis that we have at this time.'

"Now, do you understand why I don't want to go get this checkup? The cancer, it's in the family," I told Sara, not needing an answer.

THE DIAGNOSIS

L ike it or not, there I was staring at another model doctor, Doctor
   Uro, listening to his clamor, watching his face tighten with grimaces,
waiting for the worst. I didn't have long to wait.

"Your biopsy shows the beginning stages of prostate cancer; your PSA
is abnormally high. You need to come up with your own plan of attack.
There are no guarantees, but there are available treatments that can be
considered, but it must be done immediately. Doing nothing is not an
option. It won't go away," said the troubled doctor.

His prognosis didn't surprise me––it horrified me. Mentally I had tried
to prepare for it, although when I heard those concrete words, so definite,
so unchangeable, I froze. His one-sided conversation continued.

"Here are your options: laser surgery, chemotherapy, pellets. There are
pluses and minuses with any choice, but it is all laid out for you in this
designated material. Read it and get back to me." He handed me a packet
of information that I didn't remember taking. My mind was fixated on
his choice of words, my options. Wasn't he supposed to tell me what to
do? Wasn't he the medical guru? Why in the world would he want me to
decide the treatment? Anger and rage filled my mind, giving me a migraine
headache that momentarily interrupted my panic.

"If you have any concerns or questions, please don't hesitate to contact
my office," the hurried doctor said. With that he was gone like a puff of

medical smoke. Tears of fatigue leaked down my face as I sat in indecision, not knowing if I even had the strength or courage to make it home. Home meant Sara. I just knew that I had to get to her, somehow. That one realization kept me grounded until I opened the door and saw her hopeful, assured face. Maybe I shouldn't tell her right now, I thought, sensing that she would break, as if she were a fragile Dalton figurine. Were two broken souls better than one? I didn't know.

"Doctor Uro gave me this reading material on my condition and told me to read it," I said.

"And what is the reading material about?" Sara asked worriedly, noticing how carefully I was choosing my words.

"Sara, you better sit," I said, knowing that my hyper wife hated to sit, hoping that the cue would be a dead giveaway, bracing her for what she was about to hear. "I don't know how to tell you this; it just all seems so surreal. I mean, I just really wasn't expecting this."

"Expecting what," she asked, listening to her stomach kneading knots, sensing that suddenly her world would never be the same.

"I mean, haven't I been through enough already with my leg and my heart-attack and now this? Maybe God hates me; maybe he is trying to punish me for something that I have done; maybe ... I can't do it, I ..." I couldn't keep going. I just didn't care anymore. I collapsed, feeling the cancer clinging to my insides. Her drained face told me that she knew and was strangely quiet, not moving a muscle. She was so young, so beautiful, so healthy, and looked so scared, but then her arms somehow found a way around me.

"Everything is going to be all right," she said, not hearing what she was saying yet knowing she had to be strong. She couldn't believe that one person had to suffer so much. She had suffered so little. "Whatever it is, we can face it together," she said.

My ears listened yet doubted if she really knew what we would be facing. Suddenly Sara couldn't help herself, and wet tears trickled down her face. Her mind raced. She didn't want to lose me. She wouldn't lose me. What would she do if she lost me?

Cancer was one thing, but tears were quite another. Seeing Sara cry so piteously pushed me out of myself, and I pulled her to me, feeling her chest heave uncontrollably. It was a defining moment for me. More than anything I wanted Sara to be all right.

"Doctor Uro told me that I have options, that I could pick my treatment depending on how I felt once I read the literature. Here, here, this is what he gave me," I said, making myself steady, thinking that I had been hurtled into a time warp and had overheard someone else's prognosis, but I hadn't.

Taking the pamphlets, Sara spied the words dealing with prostate cancer, and her soul sank deeply, hearing imagined cries from her dying husband, her Polo who was suffering, withering away from the dreaded disease. Cancer was so headstrong, only wanting to destroy; it was unstoppable, everyone knew it, including her.

"Did the doctor tell you anything else except to read the pamphlet? What did he tell you about your particular condition?" she asked, yanking at the unknown, hoping her soul straps would keep her up.

"Right now I just want to rest. I just don't have the energy to do this. I just need some time to think and reflect on ..." I wanted to shrink into the sofa and be forgotten.

Sara wanted to shrink as well, yet she knew that she had to talk to somebody or she, too, would fade away and be forgotten. So she left. In stressful situations her mother's wisdom was like a natural tranquilizer. Right now she desperately could use one.

"Mother," she said, clenching the phone tightly while her voice broke into pieces, "it's Polo, he just returned from the doctor; it isn't good. None of it's good."

"Now hold on, tell me exactly what the doctor said," replied Edna, Sara's mother, in her matter-of-fact nurse's tone. She had been a nurse for forty years; it had consumed her, as well as her voice.

"I don't really know the details; only that Polo is clutching pamphlets on prostate cancer and wants to be alone. He just told me that he had to decide on a treatment right away, and waiting isn't an option," Sara blurted out, unable to control herself, wishing she could erase the last hour like an unwanted voice on an answering machine.

Edna knew her daughter only too well and realized that she was close to breaking. It was similar to the time in third grade when she had found her daughter hysterical, gasping for breath because her best friend had completely demolished her ambitious tree fort for no apparent reason.

But this was different. She couldn't comfort Sara over the telephone with chocolate ice cream drenched with chocolate sauce and sprinkles. Reaching her despondency was the only way to comfort her. She thrust the phone to her other half, Percy, who always had a calming effect on Polo.

"Daughter, everything is going to work out; you will see. Let me talk to Polo for a minute, all right?" said Percy to his unglued daughter.

I reluctantly took the phone and hesitated.

"Polo, I heard that you have been assigned some reading," said Percy, hoping to reassure me however he could and with whatever he knew.

"Percy, the gist of it is that I have, well, it seems that I have a disease that may not be curable; it's prostate cancer, and I just, I just don't know what I am going to do, that's all," I said.

"Polo, several of my friends have contracted the same disease and are still around to talk about how they beat it," said Percy. "From what I understand, you have to arrest the growth right away, so that it doesn't spread to other areas. Your doctor, what did he suggest that you do?" asked Percy, hoping that he sounded reassuring. He wished he could talk man to man instead of talking into the cold emptiness of the portable telephone. But it would have to do.

"Well, that's just it, he didn't suggest anything; he wants me to select my course of treatment after reviewing the various options," I replied, feeling woozy and sick to my stomach.

"Well, that sounds reasonable. I know Sara would be a good sounding board if you would allow her to help you out with this one, Polo," said Percy, wishing it wasn't what it was, remembering how he felt when he had his own scare with a high PSA count. To Percy it all seemed very untimely just when his determined daughter had made some loving inroads with her beloved professor. As Percy and Edna bent their knees as far as they would go, they prayed to their powerful Lord for mercy and divine intervention, knowing Sara and Polo now needed unwavering backup.

After my initial breakdown, I guess my professor part got the best of me. Pellets. I felt like I had selected food for a guinea pig. But that had been my choice, and now I was laid out in the doctor's office in a very compromising position. (Too bad it wasn't Sara in her ragged sweatpants after one of her quick baths. Funny, she hated baths; you might think she was half cat, she so despised getting wet.) Anyway, it wasn't. Instead an experienced nurse had prepared a tower of towels secluding my lower body while the pellet-man got himself prepared for the insertion.

"This will not be too intrusive," I heard the commanding voice say. "The anesthesia should take care of any discomfort that you might experience." It was as though I was listening to a talking textbook. Couldn't be more clinical than this, I thought, while the anesthesia spoke to me. The pellet-man's time meant money, while my time meant ... Why bother with the analogy when I may not have one. After careful consideration pellets seemed to be the best choice, although the procedure was still experimental. Chemotherapy would have been a sure bet for baldness and weight loss but not necessarily a cure. Just then I felt it, the piercing pain that wasn't supposed to happen. Cursing the pellets under my breath, I wondered if the good doctor had done any damage to other significant parts while in the neighborhood.

"Steady now, we are almost finished," the voice continued, and then I passed out. I guess I had given the unquestionable pellet-man a scare, since I wasn't supposed to have passed out for so long. Quivering and gulping, his Adam's apple said it all as he spoke with me after I emerged from my near-comatose state.

"The procedure has been successfully completed," said the doctor, looking truly relieved. "You need to rest now and take it easy. No lifting, no long periods of mental concentration, no altercations, no stress."

No life, I thought. I wondered what he wanted me to do since he had just denied me access to my everyday life. Preparing myself for a life change hadn't been in the reading material; I hadn't even considered it; could I even consider it? Now I was the one who was gulping.

"You probably haven't heard," I muttered under my breath but then said very distinctly, "I am a university professor, and you have just altered my job description. You wouldn't last one day, one hour, one minute if you were in a stress-free mode. You would be squished like an unwanted bug. Are you telling me that I might not be able to continue teaching?" I asked, getting belligerent.

"I am not telling you what you can or can't do; your body will do that all by itself. You just need to know what to expect. Chemical changes are apt to affect your moods, your ability to concentrate, and your energy level," said the doctor, looking me more squarely in the eye now that he knew I had a Ph.D. Feeling like a flag at half-mast, part of me died then and there. This was it; what was the point of beating this cancer if I couldn't live my life the way I wanted to? No confrontations. That was my middle name. Everyone respected and feared me because I never backed down. Easy going just wouldn't do. Just then the flag started rising, and my anger suddenly swelled. Too bad ripping those stupid pellets out wasn't an option, yet I considered it. Maybe I could bribe the nurse to extract them? No, there was the ethical dilemma, but what about my ethical dilemma? Get a grip, and just get home, my instinct roared, knowing this time I would need Sara's input, all of it.

Once home, surrounded by my faithful books, challenging computer, and the girl of my life, Spachey, our splotched female Himalayan who never voluntarily left my side, my thoughts exploded. Suddenly I was the main attraction of an unscheduled fire works display. Battling every day with my phantom pain was one thing, but this, this was quite another. My leg was gone, but my personality wasn't, at least not yet. My anger had saved me, making me who I was today. After I lost my leg, my anger insisted that I get married, raise two beautiful daughters, provide for my family and others, get my Ph.D., get divorced, get re-married, and survive open-heart surgery with five clogged arteries. Now, I was supposed to readily give up my anger and stress, my lifelong companions. It wasn't even an option. Suddenly the phrase dreaded cancer made sense to me. Once you have it, no one really wants to make direct eye contact with you since everyone knows its appetite: it devours you. Even if you should outlast it, there isn't much of you left. Well, Sara wasn't everyone, and I heard her quiet voice enter the room.

"Was it very painful? Did everything go smoothly?" she asked, knowing full well she had to distance herself from her husband or she would cave in like a just-baked cake taken too soon out of a hot oven. Knowing full well that I had to internalize, she waited, not wanting to disrupt the process. Studying her husband, all she could see was a propped-up figure in a wheelchair being encouraged by an overweight, overzealous nurse whose sole job was to care for her patient. His wife, his soul mate, had become insignificant. It was déjà vu. It had happened just that way five years ago when I came home from the hospital mangled from open-heart surgery. She didn't know if she could face being invisible again.

"It seemed to go well, although my pain threshold was not as high as the doctor had thought," I replied, not wanting to worry her; she didn't need to know all the gruesome details. "The doctor warned me that I should expect some changes, mentally and physically, so if I start acting differently it isn't because of you; it's because of the pellets. You need to know this now, Sara, while I still feel comfortable discussing it. You know how I am; this whole thing has really undone me, and I just need some time to sort it all out. Shutting you out is not a choice, but it may happen; things may get very bad before they get better. Regardless of what may unfold, I need to know that you are in this with me. Are you?"

The wheelchair vanished; I needed her. Without a breath of hesitation, she said, "I have always been here with you through all the buts and ifs, and nothing will alter that." She suddenly looked as if she felt heroic, prevailing against the enemy—the dreaded *c* word. Little did she know of the battle that lay ahead of her and how hard she would have to fight for both of us to survive.

MY TIMING

My timing was not the same as others; it never had been. While gazing at my taped-up boxes in my office at the university, I was keenly aware that they needed unpacking, yet they stood like dedicated soldiers guarding their contents. Within a minute I would know why.

The ringing phone jolted me.

"This is Emily Pearsons." The twang in the voice was all too familiar. It belonged to the dean of the education department, who had never played in my ballpark, wasn't aware that it existed. Certain that she needed my new course schedule, I assumed she hadn't checked her box since I had submitted it earlier that morning.

"Your course schedule needs to be revamped; I need you to teach an extra course this semester, spend more time on your research, and write more published articles," said the twang. I was completely caught off guard. Had she created her own ballpark along with new rules? Was she that clever?

"More publishing?" I queried, almost in disbelief since I had just submitted an article that had gotten the attention of the state, resulting in additional monies for our impoverished students. What was she really alluding to? I thought, feeling like a puffed-up rooster ready for the fight.

"Yes, that's right," the twang continued, "so I will send you a copy of your new schedule for your verification."

Something inside me snapped. My feathers separated.

"No, that will not be necessary. I will have my letter of resignation on your desk within the hour," I replied. Not wanting to add injury to insult, I just hung up. After thirty years of service, to be talked to in this tone of voice from a woman who was so beneath me was surreal. To be told I wasn't doing enough. I didn't want to remain another minute in a place that didn't appreciate me, so I shuffled around the boxes for the last time, remembering when I was appreciated.

As though adjusting the focus on binoculars, there I was, thirty-six years earlier, being sought out by the president of the university, a man whose reputation preceded him as did mine. That's why he wanted me, because I was accomplished, well-versed, opinionated, and most importantly, never afraid to stand up for what was right. He was insisting that I be closely interviewed, rather examined like a prized Christmas tree, by his elitist, equally-white university board members. He arranged for me to fly down to Brownsville, Texas, the poverty pocket of America. So throwing Mexican caution to the hot, humid wind, I left the University of Texas where I had just received my highly-acclaimed Ph.D., which shone brightly on my forehead like a guiding lighthouse beacon. It may have been too bright, too blinding. I was very young, twenty-five, very Mexican, very proud, and very outspoken. Remembering to relax my clenched fists, I knew that I was smarter than any of them.

At the interview there were mixed looks: over-politeness masking surprised resentment. But the more I talked, the more they listened, and their caution waned like a full moon. Very soon afterwards, I was hired as chair of the education department. However, winning over my compadres, my fellow faculty members, was a different hurdle in another arena. They just couldn't believe that I had been given the commanding reins: I was so opinionated, so ethnic, and so intent on fighting for the underdog. In spite of themselves, they eventually developed an odd respect for me. After all, I exhibited moral ethics and stood by my decisions. On one particular afternoon, an even odder respect for me mushroomed. One particular professor at one particular faculty meeting challenged me to back down, but I refused. He literally blew his cork; his blood pressure popped as he was escorted to the emergency room. After that eventful day, I was probably regarded as hazardous to your health. Even to this day, that belittling professor has nothing but silent respect for me, although he is usually conveniently absent from most faculty meetings.

Yet in the classroom, once I saw their faces, I was home and knew it. The faces were young, Mexican, proud, and wanted to conquer their poverty by getting a university-accredited education. Taking that same vow long ago, I needed to show them that it could be done, ripping through poverty, becoming anyone that they wanted to be. My colleagues never really understood the intensity of my mission; neither did my first wife for that matter. But whenever I needed to remind myself, all I had to do was close my office door, look out the window, and there walked the answer, the students.

But now the blinds were closed, and I knew if ever I were going to do it, it had to be now, so I resigned. Documenting my decision with a simple sentence in a simple, sealed envelope was one thing, but telling Sara would be quite another.

The professor thing bothered me. After all, that is what I was and always had been to her. When our eyes first met, they locked for a mere second. It was all it took. I knew then. Sara was taking one of her required education courses and just happened to wind up in the back of one of my classes, holding her student poise until that eye lock-up. Afterwards, home-baked Halloween cupcakes with extended office hours of prolonged tutoring followed, and these were more like staring contests; I melted like wax on a hot candle. My thirty-one year policy of never dating students was quickly altered. After all, she was well over twenty, a bit over thirty, and the rest just fell into place, right beside me, at the altar.

So, Sara identified me as "Doctor." In fact, she made me use my title everywhere we went, which I detested, yet I used it to appease her. Unlike my colleagues, Sara was feisty and not afraid of confronting me and often did. But later, after meeting her mother, I realized it was genetic, her stubbornness. I developed a rare, loving respect for her because of her audacity to question me. What would she think of me now if she couldn't proudly inform someone, anyone, that her husband was a lifer, a professor at the university? My questions would soon be answered.

Instinctively Sara knew that something was very wrong when she heard my Cherokee Jeep screech into the driveway. First of all, it wasn't raining, so the tires shouldn't have been screeching, and secondly, it was still fairly early in the morning, so I should've been at school. Had she misunderstood when I told her that it was Saturday but that I had to get my schedule to the dean then complete my grades?

An unaccustomed knot began to form in her easygoing stomach as my key allowed me in.

"I guess your grades didn't take that long to finish after all?" she asked, forcing words, anything, something.

"Do you remember where I put Gibe's number?" I replied, not really hearing anything but the twang. "My boxes at the university needed to be picked up and adequately stacked in whatever space of our cramped garage that Gibe could find before the day's end." Now she knew something was very wrong. First, I avoided a direct question about my classes, which was highly unprofessor-like, and second Gibe, the yardman, was never called unless there was an urgent situation like putting up the green, twinkling Christmas lights in a circular motion on the palm trees, changing hard-to-reach light bulbs, or providing camouflage in the yard by planting numerous bushes and trees. Boxes didn't fall into any of these categories.

"I am not going back; it is finished," I announced, watching her squirm.

"But you had such good ideas for your statistics class. You know, the computerized graph chart that you were going to try ..." She stopped, knowing she was talking to herself.

"I need to call Gibe," I repeated and headed for the phone. She couldn't believe this was her mission-minded husband. Could I have been switched on the way home, she wondered. Then a creeping reality almost choked her; her life seemed to have been altered without a smidgen of input from her. Terrified and stunned, she now remained silent; there was nothing more to say. An unusual Saturday quietness enveloped the house. Conversation usually bubbled out of her mouth, especially on Saturday, since it had been bottled up during her hectic work week. There was the obnoxious parent who had equated her to a teaching monster since she had assigned her lazy son tutorials, the fuse that had blown because of the Christmas lights, and the neighbor's yardman, who couldn't help but notice her sunbathing.... Her pent-up drama dimmed, losing its significance. She didn't care about the belittling parent, her long, drawn-out school hours, the glitched Christmas lights, or even the inconvenience of cozy neighbors. Now, none of it mattered.

Guilt laid her hand on me. Sara deserved to know.

"The Dean wanted me to teach more classes and thought I should be doing more publishing," I volunteered, breaking the numbing silence. "It was the way she addressed me, her degrading tone, her condesending attitude, and her constant reassessment of my work after thirty-five years and counting, from a superior who is so inferior it is laughable and ridiculous. So I told her just that and resigned."

Knowing that I detested her challenging attitude, Sara tried to be gentler than usual. "Do you think that you might need some more time to really think it through?" she asked but knew only too well that I would dismiss her well-meaning words in a Mexican instant.

"The only thinking I need to do right now is to decide which books are coming in and which are staying out," I replied.

Refusing to give up, Sara continued, querying carefully, "Do you think that the pellets have anything to do with your spontaneous decision?"

"The pellets ... well, I don't know, but it still doesn't alter anything. I'm tired of fighting: people, my leg, and now my accountability. Timing is everything, or it's nothing. Today it is everything. If nothing else, thirty-five years has taught me that one invaluable lesson ..." I stopped and pointed myself toward my study, wanting only to listen to the sounds of my timing and its repercussions. As I half-curled into my couch like Spachey, who looked like someone had taken a spatula and tossed hues of brown, black, and white on her, I internalized, truly realizing for the first time that I was no longer the adored professor whom everyone coddled and respected. My inside light had been extinguished, so I closed my eyes, praying sleep would overtake my malignant emptiness.

The following days lingered with indifference. The alarm didn't hastily awaken me with its incessant chimes, the phone stopped its abrupt clamoring, fellow colleagues didn't stop by with questions or consultations;

it was as though I had been wiped off the college map with one paw swoop. When my professor buddies didn't call, the buddy part of me grieved, yet the professor part of me understood. After all, I had left and told no one, probably violating every friendship code in the book. What had I expected? Their classes, I am sure, increased in number and size, packed to the hilt to accommodate disgruntled students who had pre-registered for my classes. Now my weight had been added to their own. Realizing this, my expectations halted. It might be months, maybe even years, before a familiar, thought-provoking voice would recharge my intellectual battery. With decisions come consequences, but this consequence was unexpected and damaged me the most.

Sara became damaged as well. Her actions, her conversation, her love screamed in defiance. Her husband, her soul-mate, had deserted her. This burden was her enemy, and she hated it. Usually this joyful time of year, Christmas, had always lifted us beyond, reconnecting us, making us stronger, more determined. But her husband of seven years had departed without a moment's notice, and what remained behind was distant and aloof. Our families made and remade holiday plans, trying to include the two of us in the festivities, but I declined, not wanting to disrupt the giving and receiving. I had nothing to give except unpleasant news and wanted nothing in return.

"Polo, don't you think it would be good for you to go and visit your brothers, sisters, and of course your nephews and nieces? What are the kids going to do without Santa's lap mesmerizing them with your edited version of the Night Before Christmas and listening to their page-long want lists? More importantly, how will they remember how the wise men found baby Jesus if you are not there to remind them? Won't you miss their questioning eyes and silent mouths?" asked Sara, hoping to ignite any ember with a Christmas spark.

I couldn't believe what I had just heard, "I can't believe that you just asked me that, the Santa thing. Don't you remember when the pellets were inserted, that the astute doctor informed me that anything or anyone that breathed and had a pulse should not be placed in my lap under any circumstances? These pellets are radioactive and can cause damage, especially in that prime location," I replied, feeling worse than ever, remembering that I was hazardous to little children and cuddly cats. Making a mental note, I vowed never to pick up Spachey, Fluffy, or Snowball again regardless of how enticingly they purred or insistently rubbed against my leg.

"I did forget, but don't you think getting out of your study and being around people who love you would do you some good?" Sara asked, getting claustrophobic every time she ventured into my study since it was so cave-like. All the blinds were always securely shut. Light of any kind was not permitted except that from the computer. Sara was positive I was allergic to light because she loved it so. Whenever I couldn't tolerate her interfering, I would ask her why she didn't go outside. She waited for her cue.

"I don't want my family or yours to see me this way, not the way I am right now. My thoughts are foggy, disconnected. The Polo everyone is so eager to see is not here. So why should I alarm everyone when I can't be who they expect?" I said, wanting Sara to realize that I wasn't going anywhere anytime soon. I just couldn't. Part of me ached because I knew how much family meant to her, especially when I was with hers. Edna was like my second mom, always encouraging me to ignore my chronic leg pain, eager for me to get out and live my life more fully. In other words, take her daughter out to dinner or somewhere else once a week, which I hardly ever did. I was always hurting too much. Edna breathed in what she breathed out, never giving into her own chronic pain: severe back spasms had twisted her, pretzel-like, hunching her over. From engagement ring to wedding band, Edna, in her own persistent way, had quietly stomped into my life, commanding my respect easily because she was born with gloves on. Now she wanted me to lace mine up, yet I didn't know where they were. Getting pumped up like a freshly-made bowl of minute popcorn on a Sunday afternoon wasn't mentally or physically possible for me. Anyhow, it wasn't Sunday. If Edna were to see me like this, she wouldn't understand. Not only would she worry about me, but also about her daughter, Sara, who was so loved. Percy would be alarmed as well Ever since Percy and I first shook hands and I felt that Yale grip, there was a connection, and I didn't have to worry about impressing him; he wasn't interested. His down-to-earth manner grabbed me and never let me go. So we became confidants, talking about this kicker and that receiver, weather patterns, and how to get along with his somewhat stubborn, compulsive yet very loving daughter. He knew her only too well. During Sara's school years,

Percy had been selected as the designated driver, but not on the road. He directed her through geometry, algebra, and beyond. How did Percy describe it? The patience that he thought he had vanished like smoke curling out of a chimney on a December day in his beloved Connecticut. Both he and Sara cherished and missed Connecticut greatly, especially in the one-hundred-plus temperatures of the sweltering, humid, choking Texas summers. In their beloved Connecticut there were the family rules, which young Sara never obeyed; instead she did what she wanted to do regardless of the consequences. There was the infamous bell that was rung and rung and rung, getting everyone's attention except Sara's. She was supposed to stay within hearing distance yet never did. Disappearing came naturally to Sara––part Indian, as Percy put it. Even today she could choose her own tribe, fitting in nicely. One minute I can be having a major conversation with her, then the next thing I know, I am talking to myself; she is nowhere to be found. Percy tried his best to pass the codes onto me, hoping I would have better luck in figuring out how she operated, but I haven't cracked the codes yet. Ordinarily I would jump at the chance to see Percy, but even his magnetic pull couldn't reach me now. The only bright lights that would be able to reach me were right in front of our house––the green, twinkling ones encircling the palm trees. To see them I just needed to pull up the shades; maybe I would, but only after Sara left. I wouldn't want to alarm her any more than I already had.

So Christmas passed, and the following weeks collided into one another. As though she were a sponge soaking up a mess, Sara absorbed her hurt and soon stopped asking her husband why and why not.

My sofa grew more comfortable with each passing day; I saw little reason to get off of it, but when I did my indentation stayed behind permanently, etched in the pliable Italian leather. All former routines that had given me a sense of balance and structure, I abolished. I saw no need to shave, primp, or even go upstairs to my roomier office. Within an arm's length was my laptop computer that now functioned as a tray, as well as being a portal to the outside world. Watches, I couldn't get enough of them. From the practical thirty dollar wristband to the absurdly impractical, ornamental timepiece. My dad had the same craving, so I guess it was genetic. It wasn't that I needed one or wanted one; that was the beauty of it. Time meant nothing to me now; that's why watches intrigued me so. Even the chance to spend quality time with family members had run out. The calling stopped. The visits stopped. I got my wish to be left alone. The pellets had succeeded in separating me from myself and others.

"Polo," I heard Sara scream joyfully in a high-pitched voice, "the white, black-tipped pelicans are back; you know the ones with the six-foot wing spans. Come quick. They are down by the lake."

I didn't budge. Ordinarily this was one of our winter rituals––to observe the gorgeous birds as they migrated through our area. Now not even the flying marathoners could entice me to move.

"You go, take the binoculars, observe their intricate landing pattern, then tell me what you saw," I replied, waiting for her to dash out, but she didn't.

"What do you mean?" she cried, running into my study. "We always go together and watch the pelicans; there must be at least fifty of them. You're telling me that you can't take five minutes to congratulate these determined birds on their successful journey from Africa and beyond?" It had always been a defining moment: the pelicans and their cries, their instinct for survival, and their emphasis on the group instead of the individual. Dwarfing our problems, the migration always put things in perspective for both of us, but I didn't care.

"You are wasting precious time," I said. Sara knew what I meant since she had been dashing in and out of the house for days, binoculars in hand as the peering neighbors lowered their blinds as fast as they could pull the cords, thinking she had developed perverted tendencies. Her heart sank as if it had gone down with a crippled boat. Only one tiny part of her remained above the surface, refusing to sink and deciding that I was going to see the pelicans one way or the other.

"I know it is an effort for you to put your leg on, but I will help, so it won't take long," she quipped, brushing by me, reaching for my leg.

"Sara, wait, slow down. Can't you just go and enjoy it for both of us?" I asked, holding back, not wanting to tell her how I really felt.

"No, we always go together," insisted Sara, watching that tiny bit of horizon disappear; then a second ritual ended abruptly.

Self-Disgust

Agonizing deep within myself, I knew that I was falling deeper where no arms could reach me, regardless of who they belonged to. The ripple of a soft voice whispered inside. The whisperer belonged to my shrink. It had been too long since I had seen him. Our last visit was connected to my greatest turmoil, my open-heart surgery when death clung to me, and its aftermath, my debilitating panic attacks.

Now as I looked at him, I felt even more clogged, as if it were rush hour on a four-lane highway. On our last visit he had tried to assure me that my arteries were now comparable to a twenty-year-old's. Hearing it and believing it were two different things.

"I remember the last time we spoke that you were trying to cope with your bypass surgery and too-often panic attacks. Today you don't seem agitated. Quite the opposite." He swept through his earmarked notes trying to reconnect himself with his patient's past issues.

"Doc, I don't feel it anymore; the drive, the need to contribute, that connection. I quit my job." I paused, watching for a flicker of disapproval, but there was none. "No one asks me for advice or assistance; no one asks me for anything. And the brightness in Sara's eyes, the only eyes that really matter, has been snuffed out ..." Almost breaking down, I choked, feeling light years beyond inadequate.

"This choice of quitting at the college was yours?" queried Doctor Franco. "I don't think I could ever forget the night before your surgery when your ungraded final exams were scattered all over your bed. Nothing would do until you graded every last one of them. How could something that was so significant become so insignificant? What happened to that professor?" he asked, sounding like he needed to know.

"Things at school changed, people changed. It was no longer fun or challenging for me. The politics got in the way. It was time. It was time for me to exit, giving someone else the opportunity to play the expected games the expected way. I just couldn't do it anymore." Looking down at the floor, I felt like I was on it. "More than that, I have pushed Sara away, pushed everyone away."

"Why have you pushed her away? Isn't that why you wanted to survive your heart operation, because of your love for her? You didn't want to leave her all alone with so few memories and so many unfulfilled dreams? You told me that Sara never left your side and even refused to let the doctors wheel you away until each one of them swore to bring you back alive and ticking. Was that a professor on the operating table, or was it a man?"

"I have always been a professor first. I was her professor, smarter than she was, and she wanted it that way. She idolized me, insisting that I use my pretentious title wherever we went, so I did. She was so proud of me, and now ... now I am no longer that professor. I am nothing, not even a man, I can't even ... I have, well, I don't have much time. Maybe six months––maybe more, maybe less; no one really knows. She needs to learn to get along without me. The more I push her away, the better it will be in the long run."

"Why do you feel that your time is running out? What are you really trying to say?"

"It's cancer, prostate cancer. When it was diagnosed, one doctor thought this, one thought that. Yet there are really no answers, just various treatments with various possibilities. No one really knows how to kill it or to prevent it from returning, rather like a nosy neighbor that keeps showing up unexpectedly on your doorstep. Having chemicals siphoned into my body, alias chemotherapy, was definitely not my choice. I opted for this fairly new treatment, radioactive pellets that are inserted into one's manly area. Their job is to release chemicals that with any luck are supposed to arrest the cancer. I am a pragmatist, and whether it is five months or five years, people around me need to start depending on themselves instead of me. Especially Sara and my overprotective sisters, who insist on giving me advice instead of concentrating on their own daily dramas, which I usually end up fixing one way or the other. But Tina, Tina is different; our connection has always been and will always be. She has never tried to meddle in my life; she wouldn't know how. She loves me purely without taking or expecting.

"Tina is your oldest sister, is that correct?"

"Yes, she is, but that isn't the reason. Our connection is based more on what we don't have than what we do. Both of us had something taken away, suddenly, permanently. When Tina was about seven, she lost her ability to speak due to some dark, traumatic incident that never showed itself, while my twenty-year-old leg was ripped off because of a drunk driver. Suffering and rejection have stalked us, uniting us. We both know what it is like to be whispered about."

"But don't you think you have become connected with Sara as well? With all that has happened to you, hasn't this brought the two of you much closer, much faster?"

"Yes, perhaps that is true, but we are connected because of circumstance, not because of need. She survived almost half a lifetime without me. Because my name just happened to appear on her class schedule as one of her professors, I met her. She was completing her teaching degree and somehow managed to get into my education class, which was supposedly full. It was purely random, purely luck. Self-reliance has always been a qualifier for me when a relationship raises its demanding head. From the beginning Sara fought it like a wild dog and still does. Figuring things out for herself is not her forte; she finds it much easier for me to fix anything and everything that happens to her on a daily basis, as though it were my job, without the pay, a twenty-four hour fix-it man."

"So, you don't want Sara to need you?"

"Will it help her? What can she look forward to other than more pain and suffering? As far as I am concerned, cancer at any stage is a signed death warrant. I need to put as much distance between myself and the others, and the sooner the better. It may strike you as odd to hear this, yet I now have a better understanding why people commit suicide; once it is over, it's over, and people have no choice but to move on. You don't have to agonize, visualizing and revisualizing your last gasp and its consequences. You are in control instead of your circumstances. I want to be the one who decides what happens to me."

"I hate to discourage you, but you aren't the type to commit suicide. You don't have a compulsive personality. You don't fit the profile."

"That may or may not be true, but last week I had it all mapped out. Choosing the rafter next to the stairwell, I realized how easy it would be to put a bowline in the cord, anchor it around my neck, and let myself simply slide off the stairs. Truthfully the only thing that prevented me from doing it was that I didn't want Sara to come home from school and find me dangling right in her face. It wouldn't be respectful, but if it didn't involve anyone else, I would do it. My self-respect is gone; it is as if it never existed."

"It surprises me that you should say that because I have nothing but the utmost respect for you. Have you ever stopped and thought, really looked at all you have accomplished when so much was stacked against you? Just the mere fact that you are Mexican-American was enough to derail you forty years ago. Don't you realize that you were a forerunner, paving the professional, ethnic path for the rest of us? At that time a Mexican-American graduating with a Ph.D. from the University of Texas, why, it was unheard of, because if you weren't white, well off, or connected, a college education was not an option, and graduate school was a mere midnight fantasy. You made the fantasy a reality for those of us who followed you. You are an inspiration to me as well as others. Not only have you overcome your ethnic and impoverished beginnings, but you did it when everyone thought your personal best would be getting out of your wheelchair, relearning how to walk. You stunned them all, achieving more than they could have ever imagined. I question if I could have done it."

I deliberately shifted in my chair, looking away, not wanting his adulation.

"Ever since I was a youngster, using my God-given abilities was an expectation, imbedded in me like a well-formed fossil. Then on the night of my accident, time shook me. One instant my life was under my command; the next it mutinied. Like an inextinguishable Olympic torch, the doctor's words today still burn in my brain. 'Son, if you plan on achieving anything in your life, you need to do it before you reach forty; otherwise it will be too late.' There was no choice for me; I had to do what I had to do, if I were going to do it, so I did it. On the other hand, my older brother Samuel, who also sustained slight injuries on that same night, in that same accident, was not given a timetable. He has never fully used what he has, and that bothers me."

"Does Samuel have heart problems?"

"No, he is pretty healthy."

"So why do you expect so much of other people? Didn't your ambition pretty nearly kill you with your five clogged arteries and severe panic attacks?"

"Well, maybe it did, but I believe what I believe; one's personal best is all that matters ... Having said that, Doc, I know that it came out of my mouth, but I don't know where that Polo is who believes it. Without asking, he has distanced himself from me."

"Isn't that what you are trying to do to those around you who love you?"

"Maybe it is the same, but I just want to be left alone. Everything seems so pointless; my punch is gone. This nothingness that I feel doesn't belong in me. I have never given up, ever. Challenges have always centered me. I welcomed them, sought them. But now, I just see no need to continue the fight."

Doc paused, knowing he had to choose the rest of his words carefully.

"Did your urologist happen to mention that the pellet treatment might change your chemical make-up, altering your moods and feelings?"

"Yes, he told me that it might happen, but to change so completely like a bright green chameleon that instantly turns dull brown, I didn't think it possible. But unlike the chameleon, I don't think I can change back. I wouldn't know how to go back. There is no back. My resentment, my determination, and my fearlessness is gone."

The good doctor commanded my attention with his clinical eyes. "Are you familiar with the term clinical depression? Your symptoms match the exact definition of this disorder, which in your case, I believe, has been caused by your radioactive pellets. The chemicals have altered your reasoning factor. Often when we have to deal with change, many changes at the same time, we lose the ability to cope. Our coping mechanism goes into neutral, and the result is that we tend to isolate ourselves and stop caring about everyday living and people whom we love. It is treatable, and help is available in different shapes and sizes."

"You are suggesting anti-depressants, tranquilizers, aren't you? Well, you already stated that I am not the addictive type, so I suppose ... When I lost my leg, the doctors gave me enough pain medication, morphine, to deaden a horse. But then six months later when the doctors suggested that I withdraw slowly, I just threw the deadeners down the commode. It was purely a case of mental gymnastics."

"This is somewhat different. It might be more difficult for you to handle since your emotions are out of alignment instead of your mangled leg. When thoughts become distorted, it is sometimes harder to balance them, harder than outwitting physical pain."

"Doc, mental illness has always been a passion of mine. Most people are ignorant of its extensions, but I didn't think that I was. During my thirty-five years of teaching, I have counseled students whose grades have suddenly dropped for no apparent reason until I talked to them, discovering that they just didn't care about grades or anything else. The more that they talked, the more I listened. They were depressed and needed professional help, so I referred them to counselors. I just never imagined that I would fit so snugly under the same label."

"It can happen to the best of us. Life takes its twists and turns, and you just have to try and hold on any way that you can. This prescription will help you do that. One is an anti-depressant, and the other is a mild tranquilizer. Take them as directed while monitoring your feelings and behavior. Start a daily journal, documenting your thoughts, how you handle things, and then examine what is on the written page. It will be second nature for you, although now it will be your own writing that you are critiquing."

"Examining my emotions is not something that I am comfortable doing. Self-reflection has never been on my agenda. Providing for others has always taken precedent. My feelings have never been important to me."

"That may be true; however, acknowledging your feelings now will be very significant; it is your way back."

I knew what he was getting at, but I wasn't sure just then if I even had any feelings except self-disgust. I guessed I would find out.

LIFTING THE VEIL

Day 1:

The pills were easy enough to take, but Sara wasn't. How could someone with her persona possibly understand how I felt when she had never faced an obstacle in her life, except perhaps deciding whether or not to marry me? No, not even then, since I had to derail her urgency, when that was all that I ever heard. Then when became now, and a date was set. It wasn't lack of dedication; it was my uncertainty. Would she be able to handle my struggles, my responsibilities to others before her entrance, her grand slam into my life? To my two beautiful, individualist daughters, I was both mother and father since a tumultuous marriage ended in chaos. I was their stability and private checking account. Sara needed to understand that concept; there wasn't extra money for extra things; there never had been. When I first met Sara, I was driving my old jalopy, my seasoned confidant of twenty years. It fit me, my profession: "a posthole digger," a Ph.D., a professor. Each time she got near it, she hyperventilated, as though she were having an allergic reaction. She probably was but assured me that it wasn't the car that she was interested in. It was the man inside of it. Funny, though, as soon as we were married, the car vanished. Before I knew it, I was driving a brand new jeep with all the latest gadgets. So much for the driver.

With Sara there were no formers, no ex-husband, no children, no complications, and no mistakes. It wasn't her fault, I guess, that she was born into a well-kept family with well-kept resources, but I wasn't, and struggle was all that I had known. I wasn't sure if Sara could enter that world, but she has and has flourished like a prized, transplanted rosebush. That just irritates me all the more. Her joy is overflowing like a gushing well from deep within. It always has been. I secretly hoped that I could drain a bit of it, but I haven't. I have never felt that kind of joy, and it makes me feel uncomfortable. I lay my pen down, realizing that now I had to go back and read it. I didn't want to; I knew how uncaring and unloving I had been. Ripping it out, I shredded it and threw it across the room as a soft tear whisked down my cheek. Tasting the salt, I wondered if maybe I did still care somewhere deep inside, in the midst of the darkness.

A quiet voice softly said, "What are you feeling? Maybe we could talk about it." Sara instinctively knew that she had to intervene, to help her husband, or else there would soon be no husband to help. All her life she had been surrounded with reassuring love; she knew what it was, how it felt. She was not going to give up, not now, not ever. It was her genetic make-up, her strength.

"Are you my shrink?" I answered indignantly, not wanting to discuss any of it.

Taking a lighter tact she replied, "You know, I did take some psychology courses in nursing school." She remembered the mental institute, the frightening bars shrouding the windows, the stone faces, and the twisted behavior. She refocused herself; visible bars were also here between them, wanting to push them apart. They couldn't. She wasn't going to allow them to, even if I did.

Her humored softness penetrated me. "You just wouldn't understand it; I don't even understand it. It is as though I have fallen head first into this high-walled pit, and there doesn't seem to be any end to it. The walls are so steep with no apparent footing. To make matters worse, I am turned around, unable to see the opening, unsure if there even is one."

"My arms are awfully long; I can reach you; just let me," she whispered.

"There is no need to even try. That Polo you want to rescue is gone. I don't know whether he will ever be back. The doctor seems to think that medication will help, tranquilizers, but I doubt it, because it only makes me groggy, masking everything like a misty, tropical rainforest. He suggested that I examine my feelings by jotting down journal entries; but none of them are worthy enough; they are stuffed full of hatred and loathing. Sara, I know that this is probably very scary and confusing for you, because it is for me. Every bit of it. I mean, how much more am I supposed to take? The chronic, crippling phantom pain, the critical heart operation, the creeping cancer, and now, now an unknown rogue (or someone else) has taken my place. Do you now understand why you can't help me? No one can." I paused, exhaling a deep breath. "You know, I wouldn't blame you if you were to leave. I would leave. It just wasn't part of the plan, the intended 'I do.'"

"But you aren't me," she muffled, turning away as her ears vibrated with my last pitiful words. Then she understood. I couldn't be her husband, because he loved her, he needed her. He would never say such a thing, even during a stubborn tug-o-war, and there had been a few. If this were an imposter, would she be able to stay the course like her father on his beloved sailboat? Comparing the two, she realized that the thing her father loved the most almost killed him. It happened one fateful day when he lost his footing, capsizing into the bowels of the ocean blue. The sails artfully wrapped their bold emblems around him, trapping him, almost suffocating him. Somehow he managed to wiggle out. Before you could ask him about the gruesome details, he sold his boat, knowing his love affair had abruptly ended. She, too, had a love affair, and it was with her husband. Her love affair wasn't going to end, not now, not ever. Her body wasn't tangled; it was her mind. She was extremely sensitive, and my last words had opened an ugly mental wound. I had to be in there somewhere, but could she find me before it was too late? This was the only thought racing through her bruised mental highways. Could she? An unaccustomed nausea swept through her doubt. As she rushed toward her bedroom, three pairs of adoring green eyes waited. There were no imposters here. Snowball, Spachey, and Fluffy, her constant feline companions, needed and wanted her love regardless of what and if. So after dry heaving and successfully saturating her pillow, she snuggled with Snowball and Fluffy, who were very supportive, while Spachey purred a warm purr that could steer any boat in any weather. It was only then that Sara knew an imposter would never defeat her.

Until that one night, though, she was never quite certain. As days grew into weeks and weeks into months, she found it harder and harder to even try. His words troubled her. His actions stopped her. She no longer knew this man who relentlessly consumed their food, hypnotically watched their TV, and vegetated on their Italian leather sofa. She often regretted that her parents had given it to him, since it was much too comfortable and much too convenient. It consumed the room, which he never left. It met all his needs: his laptop computer, TV, sofa by day, and bed by night. The imposter was thriving. But that night was different. It had all started with the phone call; she had mistakenly picked up the telephone but intentionally listened.

"I haven't seen you in so long; you never call, you never ... What happened to my brother, the one who loved me and was supposed to be there for me no matter what? I miss my brother," Tina mumbled eerily, trying to vocalize the sounds.

"I am not able to see you; I am just not strong enough to drive for an hour through all that traffic, with all of that construction. Tina, I have my own problems right now, just too many of them. You will just have to call on one of the other six to help you out if you need something. I am just too tired," answered Polo.

Sara almost dropped the phone. If Polo cared about anyone it was Tina, his older sister, whom he had idolized and taken care of all of his life because of their special connection. When Tina was five and suddenly lost her ability to speak, Polo became her angry protector, determined to find the clue; however, there were none. So she survived in a silent world with her deaf husband. Polo had always dropped anything and everything at the sound of her voice, but tonight he didn't. He was completely removed.

It sickened her. She had heard enough, too much, and laid down the phone. His callousness revolted her; the imposter had successfully stampeded another relationship, crushing the fragile heart of his most adoring fan.

I ended the phone call quickly as a voice from within me said, "It was Tina." Hearing my own voice shocked me, and I sobbed, knowing

I had just shattered an oath, one that I made to Mama on her deathbed, promising to take care of Tina until her natural end. Every nerve ending in my body cringed in horror. Mama's trust had been violated, which was unforgivable. This time he had gone too far. No one came between me and Mama, not my kids, not Sara, not my brothers or sisters, certainly not him. I knew he had to be stopped, and there was only one way to do it. There were no nightly noises coming from Sara, so I assumed she had fallen asleep, at least for a while. Sleep eluded her, three hours up and three hours down. Six months ago she welcomed sleep, looked forward to it. But now sleep had become an unwanted tease, documenting her unhappiness. Clearly, precisely, the plan took on a mind of its own. Quietly making my way to the bathroom, I listened to it. There could be no mistakes, no errors. He would not be able to figure it out until it was too late. He would be unable to stop me. I didn't need a journal to analyze this. As I carefully brushed my teeth, he stared back, mocking me, taunting me. The toothpaste turned bitter, regardless of its mint flavor and whitening powers. Ignoring him, I looked through him, and that's when I sensed it. A certain lavender, laced chilliness spread through the air, making me dizzy.

Was it the imposter? No, he was still right in front of me, but he broke his silence.

"It must be the tranquilizers or the pellets or the food. Maybe Sara poisoned it. You know, she has probably had her fill of you and come up with a plan," he said. Cleverly, very cleverly, the imposter had sensed something, as though he knew what was about to happen. I took a step backwards, wanting some distance between us, forcing my mind to stop.

What was that he said? No, Sara would never poison me, because she loved me. Startling words. But I knew love: how it connected, how it felt, how it healed. He had no idea what love was. How could he? He would never allow it. As I sorted this out, a very faint yet very persistent outline formed next to me. Panicking, I instinctively closed my eyes, demanding that it leave, but it didn't. Then its words started. Blocking them was useless because they were intense, like hurricane winds.

"Polo, it is your Mama." The lids on my eyes remained sealed. My analytical nature knew this was ridiculous, impossible since Mama had passed away thirteen years ago. However, the words kept forcing themselves, jamming my brain like a telepathic inscribed message.

"My dear Polo, listen with your heart and not your intellect. You need to hear what I have to say. What you are about to do can't happen. We are not ready for you. There is more for you to be, to love." The piercing words made their mark, so I forced my eyes open.

"Mama, if it is somehow possible, I mean if you are really here, please give me some kind of sign." Within seconds the lights flickered on and off rapidly. I gave in. Mama began to close in on me. Forbidden tears ran in rivulets down my face, drenching me. I felt them. He hadn't won yet.

"Mama, I just want to be with you and Papa. Continuing this way makes no sense. There is nothing here for me. Fighting him is useless; my desire is gone." Mama's mental embrace wrapped itself around me, encouraging me to verbalize the rest, the hardest part, the dreaded part. "Mama, I broke my promise to you. I can't be your little soldier anymore, not with Tina, not with any of them. The six of them need to take care of themselves. I can't be the one to fix them. I can't even fix myself. A veil of darkness has separated me. I can't find my way back. It is him." There, I said it. Now I could destroy him without guilt.

"Polo, he is you, you are him. There are not two of you. For some reason your ability to love, to care, to need has been blocked, but you have the power to unblock it. Sara's love for you is powerful and cannot be doubted. She needs you and has not given up. How could she when you are all she ever wanted and waited half of her life to find?"

Sara still loved me; I hadn't even considered it.

"Mama, there is something, something terminal that can't be unblocked. I have, I have cancer, and it is just a matter of time. I want to be the one who determines when and how I go."

"Is that what you think? That you still have the cancer? It has been over a year since your diagnosis. Have you been tested recently?"

"Well, no, I canceled my last appointment. It's all too obvious. I don't need to be told exactly how many months I may or may not have left."

"That surprises me since you have always been a factual person. Your whole life has been based on the facts: your family, your Mexican pride, your poverty, your desire to matter, your Ph.D. Are you telling me now that facts don't interest you? Well, this fact will. Your cancer is in remission, and a lab test will document it. So your natural end is nowhere in sight."

I was sure I had misunderstood that last fact. Could it really be that I wasn't dying? It was numbing. All this anguish, all this time. He knew it and assumed that I wouldn't find out. But wait, Mama just said that we are one in the same. So now we both know, so maybe now I don't need to ...

"Mama, even if this is true, I don't know if I am strong enough to fight again, to try again."

"I guess that will be your plan then, to try and find out. Always know that with love, there is hope. My son, my love for you is eternal, and nothing in your world or mine will ever change that."

Abruptly the messages stopped. The lavender-smelling coldness disappeared. Reaching, I grabbed at air, grabbed at anything, but nothing was there. It didn't matter; I could feel her with me.

My plan suddenly became obsolete. Looking deeply into the mirror, he did as well. I looked for his mocking grin, his challenging eyes, his carelessness, but they were gone. Filled with urgency, I couldn't wait to tell Sara the impossible.

"Sara, Sara!" I frantically shouted. "It's gone. Mama just told me it is gone." I trembled like jelling jello.

Hearing my fitful cries, Sara ejected herself from an exhausting dream: teaching a new class of students who refused to be quiet. Stumbling down the hallway, she focused on something she hadn't seen for a very long time. It was someone who looked like her husband coming toward her instead of going the opposite direction. Was this dream a wanted one? She kept looking, and it was her husband. But something was different. Everything was different. He was emotional, vulnerable. Reaching him, she looked directly into his eyes. His frozen stare had thawed.

"Do you still love me? Do you?" I asked, hoping against hope that Mama had been sending me the correct signals. I certainly didn't want to be humiliated now, at least not until I told her.

Quivering as much as me, Sara answered, "My love for you cannot be questioned, cannot be interrupted, cannot be emptied. I thought you understood. What happened; why were you yelling? Were you making sure that I hadn't left?"

"Partly, but no, it's him. I don't need to destroy him; I have conquered him. He is part of me. I now know that. But the critical thing, the life-threatening thing has been stopped. The crouching cancer that has been playing hide-and-seek in my body has been annihilated, untying many laced-up terrors and knotted love. Mama told me."

"Polo, you just said that your Mama ... your Mama has been dead for thirteen years; she died right before I met you. Is that really what you meant to say?"

"I realize that it sounds bizarre, even to me, but I just had this mental-telepathic conversation with Mama. She wouldn't even wait until I finished brushing my teeth, insisting that I was indeed cancer-free. I believed her. I never told you, but I canceled my last appointment. I mean, I didn't think it mattered; two months, six months, a year. How much time I did or didn't have. But now I have time. We have time. I have been given a second chance. Do we have a chance?"

As she listened to me, it was as if a script had been written just for her. She wouldn't dare have changed one word of it. Well, maybe the Mama part, but she believed in angels, and Mama certainly qualified. My honest words strangled all of her doubts, squishing them to bits. At long last, this man, her live-in rommate, seemed familiar, seemed hopeful, seemed caring. Could her own terror be ending? Was this the man she longed for?

At that precise moment, mimicking notes of a mocking bird interrupted the script as if on cue. As I listened intently, I knew this time that I didn't need courage to go out into the night alone. I needed courage to face myself, to face my life, to face the secret of Sara's deep, ever-flowing inner happiness, to face her God. Trailing the notes, I took a deep, brisk gulp of air, fully aware that I had almost lost everything––a heart that needed my heart. Why had I been singled out? A freak accident, a lost leg, a crippling first marriage, a clogged heart, and a potentially malignant cancer all did their best to destroy me. I didn't know. It didn't matter. I was also singled out to survive.

Slowly, gently the darkened veil lifted as the pale light of the stars shone through. Sara's face revealed a determined love that refused to be silenced. We had been given a second chance. There would be a tomorrow, many tomorrows with her by my side. I knew then that I could find my way back.

Printed in the United States
By Bookmasters